Bound
for Success

NANCY FOREMAN

A Fireside Book
Published by Simon & Schuster, Inc.
New York

Designed by Barbara M. Marks
Manufactured in the United States of America

1 3 5 7 9 10 8 6 4 2

Library of Congress Cataloging in Publication Data

Foreman, Nancy.
Bound for success.
"A Fireside book."
1. Success. I. Title.
BF637.S8F6 1985   158'.1   85–1723

ISBN: 0–671–55547–2

Acknowledgments

I would like to express special thanks to the following, without whom this book would never have been written.

Deborah Chiel, for believing that I could write my own book.

Barbara Gess, whose superb editing, patience, encouragement, and support taught me more about writing than I ever learned in the classroom.

Susan Roth, for her invaluable contribution of research and background materials.

Leonard Franklin, for expertly guiding me through the literary legal forest.

Bill Adler, for accepting the challenge of my project.

NBC News; WKBW-TV, Buffalo, New York; WCPO-TV, Cincinnati, Ohio; KOLN-TV, Lincoln, Nebraska, for providing me with a landscape of high achievers and a lifetime of possibilities.

The high achievers whose stories appear in this book. During the long months of writing, they provided silent encouragement, support, and inspiration.

My husband and sons, for their unfailing understanding and patience during evenings, weekends, and holidays of writing.

To Roger,

*who has enriched this book
and my life beyond words,
and whose contribution,
both technical and inspirational,
appears on every page.*

Contents

1

♦

How I Grew
Big Ideas

SOME LITTLE GIRLS are captured by lovely dolls, frilly dresses, or tea parties and rocking chairs. I was fascinated by successful people. My dolls would go hungry while I listened to stories of the very wealthy. The tea grew cold while I went to the movies to watch Betty Grable and Esther Williams. The ruffled dresses would only be appropriate if I could wear them to the faraway palaces I clicked up on the tiny screen of my View-Master. I was hungry to know why some people became so successful. What made them different? I wanted to know what they did, what they knew, what they thought, ate, wore, read, where they went, what they listened to. No one knew what a "role model" was, but I knew that I wanted to live like them. It didn't matter whether they were men or women—success didn't know the difference. In my young mind I was trying to figure out how to do that. I knew it wouldn't be easy in Creighton, Nebraska, where Main Street was four blocks long and the link to the outside world was the radio, movies, and the Greyhound bus.

I guess I started pretty early tackling decisions that would begin to determine the direction of my life. I must have been around three or four the first time my Aunt Effie shooed the chickens out of the outhouse so I could perch on the precipice of the third hole, holding my breath so as not to inhale the ghastly odors and hanging on for dear life. I was terrified that I might fall in or that Aunt Effie's mean rooster would seek me out when I was "trapped" and couldn't run away. Then and there I decided that the first step toward success would be to have indoor plumbing! Town people had indoor plumbing, and I never took it for granted after that. I would definitely live in town where there was city water and sewers. I suppose that was a kind of goal. Although far from lofty, it most certainly was long-term and firmly placed in my mind.

Besides indoor plumbing, it was clear that an education was an entree to success. Good grades and being quiet brought gold stars and Hershey bars, but there was a very thin line between intelligence and "acting smart." That meant your good work had "gone to your head," that your appropriate modesty had given way to brash confidence and carefree behavior. And nobody liked someone who "acted smart."

I was in junior high school by the time television reached Nebraska. When there was any picture at all, the reception was snowy and intermittent. Appearing on network television, working with well-known television performers and news personnel, and living in New York City was as probable for me as being invited to step into a glass slipper that fit perfectly. I came to regard those people on television as somehow special, privileged. The women on early television were the June Taylor Dancers or the luscious beauties who introduced *The Jackie Gleason Show;* they were the silent lovelies who pulled back the curtain to reveal the grand prize of the boat or Cadillac. They looked so happy and beautiful. I wanted to be like them, but I didn't know how.

In fall 1959, I entered Stephens College for Women in Columbia, Missouri, a ten-hour drive from my hometown. It could have been on the other side of the world! My bobby socks rolled down into plump doughnuts were all wrong, and I was shocked to meet girls from Texas, California, Georgia, all over the country, who got along very nicely "acting smart."

They seemed friendly all right, but they were so "forward." My socks weren't the only thing out of style—my style was out of style! What a total revelation Stephens was for me! It was my first look at the larger world—only one state away. I struggled with my first checking account, sighed as I arranged my homely sweaters next to my roommate's genuine cashmere collection, and was intrigued to meet girls whose fathers didn't work in a store or a farm but who actually spent their working hours on a phone managing investments.

I'd never heard a live symphony orchestra, only marching bands. I had never heard of bagels and lox, Nietzsche, or Anheuser-Busch.

One year of tasting the outside world was all my parents were willing to pay for. I was returned to the safety of the University of Nebraska, where I remained until I graduated in 1963. I pledged a sorority, ratted my hair into a beehive, dressed for dinner on Monday nights, filled my calendar with fraternity dates, memorized the Chi Omega history and songs, and joined the college crowds at football games, house parties, and "beer busts." Studies were hardly an interference. I did reasonably well, but grades were clearly not a priority. Getting your boyfriend's fraternity pin was a priority. Upperclasswomen who were "pinned" or wore an engagement ring enjoyed a social position a notch above the rest of us. I got pinned to Bill at the end of my sophomore year. He was a year ahead of me, a serious student with plans to enter graduate school, and he was from Chicago. That meant indoor plumbing!

My interest in successful people remained, but the image of success for myself had been diluted and blended with the expectations of society, campus, and parents. Deep down I knew I wanted to be successful, special, but I wasn't strong enough, aware enough, or tough enough to buck the tremendous force of tradition. So I settled down to study for finals, enjoying my status of "newly pinned," when Mother phoned to give me the news that the Albion Junior Chamber of Commerce had selected me to represent the town at the Miss Nebraska Pageant the following week! I longed to float down the ramp in an iridescent ball gown, with the spotlights crisscrossing above, but I was short, lacked polish, and needed "filling out" (translation: I needed a larger bust). In June 1961, with a week of final examinations and a new pinmate, the timing was all wrong. The bustline wasn't great yet, either, but I had learned how to "carry" myself. Mother pushed, insisting that I give it a try. She would pitch in.

I had been preparing a dramatic reading as a part of a speech-class final. That quickly became my presentation for the talent competition. While I rehearsed "The White Cliffs of Dover," Mother shortened skirts and took tucks in dresses we had taken out on approval from the Albion Dress Shoppe. Then we took turns sewing sequins on an old prom dress for the evening-gown competition.

I pulled out all my visions of how a Miss Someone would smile, walk, sit, and speak, and at the end of the week when I glided down the ramp wearing the state crown, carrying two dozen red roses, it didn't matter that it was in the Fairbury High School gymnasium and that it was a dripping 103 degrees (no fans), and that I was the shortest woman to ever win the state title. It was a big moment in my life, a proud event, and just as thrilling as I ever dreamed it could be.

Atlantic City and the Miss America Pageant were like a dream come true. I had no illusions about my chances of winning. The pageant was populated by pros, all taller than I. Miss Missouri, the girl I had to stand next to in the "line up," was six feet tall, had been performing part-time in a night club, and had a bosom that held up her strapless gown with no stays. The winner, Miss North Carolina, was a former Radio City Rockette, who even on the first day wore her burgundy pillbox hat like a crown.

I did harbor the illusion that talent scouts were everywhere and that fabulous opportunities could come just from appearing in the Miss America Pageant.

However, back at the University of Nebraska, the phone lines weren't jammed with calls from New York talent agents looking for a five-foot-two midwesterner who could recite "The White Cliffs of Dover," so I settled down to making local appearances, keeping up my studies, and the next best offer: marriage.

When I placed the Miss Nebraska crown on the head of my successor, Mary Lee Jepsen, who twirled a fire baton, I was wearing a three-quarter-karat diamond solitaire and thinking about china and silver patterns. I was trying to figure out how I could manage my heavy course load, keep my grades up, and work as a student teacher when KOLN-TV called to see if I would be interested in "sitting in" with Jolly Joe Martin, a well-known Nebraska disc jockey, on a live, late-night television talk show they were trying out. I was to just be there, look pretty, give Joe (and the viewers) something to look at when the guests got boring, and to occasionally let them know that I was having a good time. It sounded great, until I discovered that the program was to air from 10:30–12:00 P.M. That's bad news for a college girl carrying a heavy class load. But it paid $5 a show and it offered the rare opportunity to work in *live* television, the kind that could only happen in a small-town television station in 1962. I had to give it a try.

The Joe Martin Show was truly an ambitious program effort. There would be ninety minutes of live programming, and that was pre-videotape, so there were no slick little video clips or syndicated television segments to pick up the pace. Lincoln, Nebraska, the state capital and the home of the University of Nebraska, is a college town and does not exactly beckon to celebrities, attract major author tours, or serve as the crossroads of American theater. What's more, Jolly Joe turned out to be a sad, melancholy man with a voice you could spread on toast. His personality, which came across very well between recordings on radio, was different from what was required for a live television program. My personality had not emerged for either radio or television. So we made quite a pair—a bland blonde and an aging disc jockey, stumbling and mumbling with no script, no routine sheet, only a card with the names of our guests. No station today would attempt such a production with such an unlikely pair. Of course, there were no television consultants in 1962 to "analyze the chemistry" between the on-air hosts. There was no chemistry, and worse, there was no place to hide. Joe was so radio-oriented that when he began playing Frank Sinatra records, he actually "acted out" on camera. He'd light up a cigarette and mime the "feelings" of the songs. Mostly he did lovesick, despair, and heartbreak in three minutes, and all looked the same. It was deadly television, but *The Joe Martin Show* was a golden opportunity. I got my feet wet in television, actually worked inside a television station, and learned what it felt like to be in front of the camera.

I left *The Joe Martin Show* two months before my December 22 picture-book wedding. It was Christmastime, but I didn't want Christmas to dominate *my* wedding. Instead, I selected flowers, dresses, and mints in shades of pale lavender. The swatches in the book looked elegant, but at the wedding, lined up in the baskets and down the aisle, lavender came across as cool, lifeless, faded, and forgettable—the color of December, of Albion, of the marriage.

December 22 was the shortest, darkest day of the year. My sorority sister Becky Schneider sang "The Lord's Prayer" and "Because." The sky darkened and it started to snow as the last guest went through the receiving line into the church basement, where the wedding cake—perched on top of a now-limp lavender net tablecloth—awaited the bride and groom. The little lavender-flowered mints that we'd ordered early and kept in the freezer had turned into the most unappealing shapes and colors, but all the gifts displayed on a long table nearby offered livelier decoration. The only person who got a look at my "going away" suit with matching hat was the photographer. Everyone else, with cake wrapped in wedding napkins, headed off to beat the storm. I wore my hat all the way to Omaha, where we would spend our first night, and wondered when I would start feeling different. That was one of the disappointing things about marriage, I thought I was supposed to feel different; I thought something was supposed to change.

Bill had secured a military deferment to complete his MBA at Northwestern, but deferments don't last forever. Six months after we were married we reported for nine weeks of officers' training at the U.S. Army Ordnance School at the Aberdeen Proving Grounds in Maryland. I found out there was more to ROTC than the military ball (the social highlight of the year at the University of Nebraska). As I scanned the grim landscape of olive-green buildings, I realized that at Aberdeen I wouldn't be needing my ball gowns or metallic gold slippers. Everything was "issue," from the haircuts to the doctors. My life turned to army drab.

After Aberdeen there were seven weeks of specialized training at the supply school in Fort Lee, Virginia. I would like to think that, although far from being a model military wife, I adapted to army life. I was proud of Bill's commitment and respected his decision, but I kept wondering what that had to do with me. I had not chosen a hitch in the military, yet there I was, expected to conform to the same system and assume the same rank as my husband. However, I definitely did not feel like a second lieutenant. I was a former Miss Nebraska, and I had a college degree . . . not the type who relished standing over an ironing board crisping up fatigue uniforms with spray starch for an inspection that wasn't even mine! I devoted evenings to smearing Brasso on insignias and spit-polishing combat boots, because I thought it was my duty. Frankly, Bill was so exhausted by the "forced marches" and bivouacs that I felt sorry for him, and I knew if we were going to have any laughs at all, I had to pitch in and try to make things easier. The best news was that we were to be permanently assigned to Colorado Springs.

Fort Carson, Colorado, was like any other army post, but the Rocky Mountains loomed majestically to the west, and we were only a ten-hour drive to my hometown. We found a furnished hillside apartment off the post that overlooked Cheyenne Mountain, with the famous Broadmoor Hotel nestled at the foot. It was a walk-out basement with three rooms of plastic, western-style furniture. A washer in the bathroom and a clothesline out back . . . all for $90 a month. With a view like that, who could complain? We barely unpacked the wedding gifts when Bill's commanding officer sent him on "TDY," a temporary assignment in Rock Island, Illinois. I immediately found my way to the Department of Education and applied for a teaching job. Only a year out of college, and already I was turning to my "fallback" profession. The life of an army wife may have been grim, but life as a speech teacher at Wasson High School was worse. I had just turned twenty-three, I stood five feet two, and most of my clothes were college carry-overs: there was no money for "image" dressing. Since I blended right in with Wasson's 2,700 high-school students, I dished out tough assignments in order to be taken seriously and argued with the hall monitors, who wouldn't believe I was really a teacher. I fell asleep grading papers each night, I dreaded lunchroom duty, developed an aversion to speeches entitled "How to Ski," "The Beatles," and "How to Bathe Your Pet." The head of Wasson's English Department, a tough old veteran who miraculously kept her delight in Keats and Longfellow, offered consolation: "My dear, you will muddle through this just like the rest of us." Success would have to wait.

The next fall when I reported for a preterm teacher meeting and classroom preparation, I noticed that the smell of the newly waxed floors nauseated me, along with eraser dust, lesson plans, and the conjugation of verbs. I was repulsed by the pungence of thirty-three teenagers packed in a classroom, all with acute hormone imbalances. I had little patience with their emotional peaks and valleys, their painful transition to adulthood, and their need to push each other into walls, chairs, and open lockers. I had my own frustrations and problems—the least of which was that I was pregnant.

It had been Bill's grand plan to have a child before he left the military. That way all the medical costs would be covered, and we would have completed an important event on schedule. I was in agreement, as I was with most things then. Little did I know that I would be plagued with morning sickness every day for the duration of the pregnancy. I grew enormous and uncomfortable, but I trooped into the post infirmary for my regular checkups. After all, I told myself, I was a big girl now and millions of women have babies in military hospitals. It was a natural, routine procedure; there was nothing to fear. The due date passed, my blood pressure went up, and at ten days overdue my physician, Dr. Mooney, announced that I had toxemia and would be hospitalized immediately.

What followed was a nightmare that "never happens in

modern maternity wards." My labor was intermittent; it had to be induced with a drug that caused violent uterine contractions. The baby was "posterior." The labor-inducing drug caused serious vomiting and dehydration. Nothing was going according to "regulation." After twelve hours of hard labor, I was pushed into the X-ray department, where the night staff captured every stage and angle of the minute-long contractions. Finally, Captain Mooney attempted a "high forceps" delivery, which failed.

Bill was informed that we would be calling in a specialist. An emergency cesarean section was scheduled for 7:30 A.M. I pleaded for it immediately. I had been in hard labor for twenty hours. I was exhausted, thirsty, my eyes were black holes from the battle that waged in my body. One look at Bill's face when he came into the labor room and I knew the situation was grave. Weeks later he revealed that he had been told there might not be a chance to save both mother and baby. Which would he choose?

It was important to keep the labor contractions working. I counted down the minutes and sucked on gauze soaked in ice water. Finally, at 7:30 A.M. I was wheeled to the O.R. right into a traffic jam! There in the corridor were rows of beds waiting for an operating room! That's when I nearly gave up. Finally, on April 28, 1965, after thirty-three hours of labor and an hour and a half wait for surgery, Jeffrey was born, furious over his shabby welcome to life.

Friends said that we had grounds for malpractice. Mother said it never would have happened that way if she had been there. Bill said he had never been so worried in his life. I was just happy to have Jeff and me alive, and that the surgery scar was a low bikini line instead of a nasty vertical scar down my abdomen.

There was little time to contemplate the scar, however. Bill was discharged from the army in June, and we moved, with a six-week-old baby, to Cincinnati, Ohio, where Bill would begin civilian life in a large consumer-products company. I stayed busy ironing Bill's white oxford-cloth business shirts, finding my way to the used-furniture stores on the fringes of the city, and being a mommy. My year as Miss

Nebraska and appearances on *The Joe Martin Show* seemed
far away. When would success get around to me?

Bill had his own burdens, worse than mine. He had to
survive in a very competitive corporate jungle where young
MBA's were chewed up and spit out by the dozens. He had
a wife and child to support, and he had to deal with the terror
of failure. We never talked about our fears, or angers, just
our goal (actually his), which was a positive personnel review
and the raise or promotion it represented. We lived from raise
to raise, and began saving for a home which became the focus
of our efforts. Meanwhile, I budgeted carefully and walked
around the parking lot of our apartment building with Jeff
in his stroller. Soon I became an expert in toilet training, encouraged by the knowledge that no one I knew had ever
failed to learn that important social skill.

When Bill came home and announced that we would be
sent on sales training in "the field," we splurged on a bottle of
cheap champagne. The fact that Jeff was only eighteen months
old, and that the "field" was Flint, Michigan, on the doorstep
of winter, did not dim our jubilation.

We barely got the U-Haul unloaded in Flint when the
snow started to fall. During those snowed-in months with a
lively toddler I became a virtual craft shop. I produced enough
candles for a lifetime . . . all colors and fragrances. Every
coffee can within ten miles became a melting pot for a new
color. When the coffee cans ran out I made burlap placemats,
hand-fringing all the edges and spraying them with Scotch-
gard. Then I hemmed coordinated print napkins. I knitted
sweaters, mittens, headbands, scarves, and hats. I made little
short-pants outfits for Jeff and took the suspenders to the
neighbor lady to help me with the buttonholes. I made several
outfits for myself, dyed my hair sable brown, bought a natural
strawberry-blond wig, and transformed the kitchen into a
decoupage studio. I collected cigar boxes, cookie cans, anything magazine pictures would stick to; then I distressed,
glued, and shellacked them. I wrote long letters to friends and
family describing the joys of sales training in Flint, Michigan.
Production stopped, however, when Jeff's temperature shot
up to 104 degrees.

The doctor in the emergency room said I was keeping him too warm in his snowsuit, and that it was just a virus. Jeff broke out in a fiery rash, and I found another physician who promptly diagnosed it as German measles. About the time Jeff recovered, our sales-training period ended.

Back in Cincinnati our regular pediatrician noticed my nervousness and asked how often I got a break from the apartment. He prescribed getting out with my husband alone at least every other weekend. It was wonderful: he gave me permission to get away for a while. He assumed the guilt that would have been mine: I was so grateful. I even contacted a local modeling agency and qualified for certain public-relations assignments. Occasionally I got a call for a job that sounded interesting. It depended on how badly I needed to get out of the house. One particularly desperate rainy March I agreed to ten days at the automobile show at the convention center, demonstrating, in a silver miniskirt, the car of the future. It paid twenty dollars a day. If the fee covered the babysitter and parking, I considered myself ahead.

Jeff was about two when we began looking for a small, affordable home. He needed a yard and neighbor children, and I needed more projects. The little ranch house at the end of the cul-de-sac for $27,500 was perfect. It offered growing room, a good school district, and a neighborhood that was appreciating. Back to the used-furniture stores. I spray-painted wicker furniture, designed and made new cushions, made curtains, planted geraniums, baked fruitcakes, fought wax buildup, and, since we still had only one car, arranged all my errands and appointments on Wednesdays and Fridays, my days to use the car. I shined the silver wedding gifts and got out the Rosenthal china. It was time to learn the art of entertaining. We were getting too old for the army beer and poker parties.

It was also time to start thinking about another child. The birth of William junior was an uncomplicated, normal cesarean section. He was a joy—slept, ate, laughed right on schedule. It was clear from the outset, however, that the two boys wouldn't be "friends." One child often invited company to play, two drew a crowd. Our sandpile became the center for stray dogs, cats, and kids, and I became the referee for all the fights. On a heavy day all my kitchen utensils would end up in the sandpile. I lost an entire set of soup spoons, measuring cups, and strainers. I made Kool-Aid popsicles in ice trays, kept the Band-Aids handy, and ruled that everyone had to return to his or her own home to use the bathroom (but they could have a drink of water from the kitchen).

For all the hassles and hard work, I wouldn't have missed it for the world. There is nothing like the virgin delight of a child making his own Halloween pumpkin, the glee of his finding the Easter basket, or the pain of a crumbling, fragile little ego over a preschool peer rejection. The first tooth, the first nursery rhyme, the school play and band concerts, the bright smile when he spots Mom, and the warm, sweet bundle of jammies that crawls into the big bed in the middle of the night for reassurance.

As the boys grew, and Bill's salary increased, we began looking for more space. Our search ended at the end of a half-mile hike through a muddy cornfield. The line of trees opened up into a glorious daisy-filled meadow crowned with an elegantly curling sassafras tree and bounded by honeysuckle and wild blackberry bushes. There was a woods sloping down to a stream . . . seven and a half acres of a dream come true. And the project of a lifetime . . . building an access road, building a cistern, building a house!

It was a battle with every stroke of the bulldozer, every shingle, every strip of molding and roll of wallpaper. There was a trucking strike, bad weather, and a temperamental builder. The new house wasn't completed by the time we had to move out of our cozy subdivision, and for six weeks we found ourselves without a place to live.

During the year spent negotiating with plumbing contractors and carpet suppliers, something very important happened. I developed a comprehensive working knowledge of the building business. My father had been a lumber dealer all his life, so I felt comfortable around the business as I rediscovered knowledge I hadn't used for years. By the time the house was half-completed I had acquired a working relation-

ship with most of the subcontractors and suppliers, and I knew
their product lines and prices as well as they did.

One day our architect said, "Nancy, why don't you consider helping some of our clients who need to be briefed on
fixtures and material selections? You would save us a lot of
time, and you could really help them make some tough decisions. You know the merchandise choices and prices, and
you've got a good eye for space and color."

Again, the timing was all wrong; I had our own house
to worry about. But it was a unique opportunity to do something I really enjoyed. Imagine, getting paid an hourly fee to
advise other people's projects. I was free to schedule consulta-
tions during the boys' school hours or whenever it was con-
venient. I agreed to start with one or two clients and see how
we all felt about it.

The architects had converted an older home into their
offices. The storeroom was transformed into my working space,
and soon samples of bricks, Formica chips, shingles, paint
charts, wood paneling, and wallpaper books lined the walls—
all the textures and colors I loved. I hung plants, ordered
business stationery, and hired a sign painter to paint a
"shingle" that would hang beneath those of the three architects. In stylized lettering on a bright yellow background, it
read NANCY UNLIMITED. The sign announced just as
plainly as a radio commercial that I was searching for my own
goal and a form of expression that could be measured in terms
other than family approval.

Each day after dropping Billy off at nursery school, I went
to my little office or to the homes I was working on. As the
business grew, time became my biggest problem, for Billy's
school was dismissed at eleven-thirty. A couple of times I got
caught in traffic and arrived at Tiny Tot Nursery School very
late. The sight of one lone, little four-year-old waiting on the
steps of the deserted school with an exasperated teacher generated enough guilt to cancel out the morning's sense of accomplishment. While Billy took his nap, I made phone calls,
typed client orders and invoices, and planned the precious
two hours I would have for meetings the next morning.

Nancy Unlimited gave me a new confidence in my abilities and my potential as a professional. It affirmed me as a person—an individual—and opened new vistas, new possibilities. When one client insisted that I consider opening my own shop and offered to bankroll the business, I realized that it was time to decide: either I make a serious commitment to the interior/exterior design business or consider other alternatives.

The interior design business, while a wonderful introduction to the working world, was very unstable, required additional capital, and was influenced by economic cycles and the real estate market. I would be competing with old, established design groups in Cincinnati, and the fact was that I had no formal training in the business. I knew I could "catch up," but did I want to invest my time and money in this particular business? At best I would be working out other people's problems and preferences, hassling slow suppliers, and making a constant effort to please others. I now had the confidence to explore what I really wanted. Success wouldn't wait much longer.

Nancy Unlimited wanted a life unlimited. I wanted to learn about everything, wanted to get to know successful people, those on their way to the top and those already there. What type of work could provide continual learning, a constant flow of interesting, exciting people, while employing my particular skills and talents?

Television met all the criteria. My limited exposure via *The Joe Martin Show* in Lincoln, Nebraska, in 1962 could hardly be considered experience. But it was a start. A career in TV, one of *the* most competitive businesses, would be a long shot, but what was there to lose? And what was there to gain? A life unlimited!

At thirty-six I was bound for success. It finally dawned on me that my life was close to half-over, and I had been a wallflower at my own party. I decided to go for it.

Through persistence and hard work, I landed a terrific job at WCPO-TV in Cincinnati hosting a new local interview program, *In Person*. My career plan was proceeding beautifully, but my marriage was rapidly deteriorating. Bill and I agreed on a trial separation only six months after I began at WCPO-TV.

There were no dramatic circumstances surrounding the decline of our marriage, no torrid love affairs or ugly scenes or bitterness. The marriage died a natural death, expiring by breaths daily over fourteen years. When I began to critically assess my life, I faced the sad truth that whatever bond there had been in our relationship was simply not there anymore. The trial separation, followed by a divorce six months later, was no easier than if there had been some crisis; it was sad, painful, and created an upheaval that was a surprise to both of us. To make matters worse, Jeff, then twelve, decided to live with Bill. However, since my new apartment was nearby, shuttling both boys back and forth for a "shared" arrangement was only a minor logistical problem. The emotional shuttling was wrenching.

Trying to manage my job, which was extremely demanding, continuing to function as a competent mother-homemaker, and dismantling a fourteen-year marriage at the same time were a struggle. But I threw myself into my work and insisted to Bill that we maintain an equilibrium for the sake of the boys. Late at night I baked chocolate-chip cookies, laid out school clothes, and planned birthday parties. I wanted the basics to continue just as they had in the past. In spite of experiencing low-grade nausea for nearly a year, and living in bone-chilling fear of my risky future, I knew I was doing the right thing for all of us.

Whatever career confidence I had darkened when, three weeks after the divorce was final, the program I was hosting was canceled and I was "reassigned" to the news department. The rumor, discreetly shared with me, was that I would not be renewed. I tried to control my panic. The financial arrangement of our divorce took my salary into consideration and provided child-support payment and short-term alimony that by itself was not enough for Billy and me to live on.

Just as I was seriously contemplating life as a short-order cook, Roger came into my life. He had been a guest on *In Person* and I remembered that he had offered to help. It was one of those general "if I can ever give you any help with anything, give me a call" promises, and a lot of people said things like that, but now I really needed help—a special kind of help. At the time, Roger was a professor and administrator at the University of Cincinnati and a consultant to CBS for children's programming. During the course of our preinterview discussion, he casually mentioned that he had been recently divorced. I was keeping my marital change quiet and had chosen to shut it out of my job completely. However, Roger, who was also a perceptive psychologist, soon had me confiding all my pain and panic to him.

When it looked like I would be out of a job, I phoned Roger to invite him to meet me for lunch and discuss whatever possibilities there might be for me in television or, for that matter, anything that would pay a regular salary. I was appalled at the prospect of actually calling a man for lunch. I had grown up with the rule that a nice girl never calls a boy. But this was 1977 and it was acceptable for a woman to be more assertive. Besides, when it's sink or swim time, baby, you grab every life raft you can find.

I was nervous when I dialed Roger's number. He hesitantly accepted my invitation for lunch the following week. But the day before he called to say that his daughter had come down with an ear infection, and could he beg off this time? As I sympathetically assured him that I understood the trials of single parenting, his daughter's voice pierced through the background: "Daddy, can Sara stay for lunch today? We want to have a picnic on the porch."

It was just too ludicrous. How could he have been such a bum? To make up a phony excuse about his daughter's illness so he didn't have to have lunch with me. Was I so bad? Would it be awkward when I offered to pay for lunch? Did I telegraph too much raw desperation? I was shattered. Being single again was very uncomfortable and foreign to me. Working with men on a professional basis was no problem, but I was unnerved by these mixed business/social situations.

When Roger called back in a few days to suggest dinner and career options, I was very cool. But I still needed help, so I politely accepted. Months later Roger confessed that he had canceled our original lunch date because he'd felt unsure and frightened. He was just as tentative and distrustful as I was and really had to get his courage up before accepting our "noninterview" meeting.

Our dinner was delightful. Roger was funny, interesting, and sympathetic. It was the first time I had opened up to anyone, and it felt good to share the pain and liberation of divorce with someone who had been there. He talked about audition tapes and talent changes in other markets. Other markets! That was the first mention of the high turnover and market-hopping common to television. After dinner Roger suggested that we get down to work and begin revising and updating my resume. That was the beginning of a full-scale career, a friendship, and later a marriage that would be full of adventure and discovery, that would grow with each of us and bring emotional shelter and nurturing to two high achievers.

The resume we drafted that night was more impressive than the one I had presented to WCPO-TV the year before. It was startling to see how much experience had been packed into one year. And that was only the beginning! Granted resumes are woefully inadequate when it comes to revealing the real you, but they do provide a chronology of major events. Using the form of a resume, let me give you some idea of how quickly my life began to soar—both up and down.

1977

January: WCPO-TV Cincinnati, Ohio (Scripps-Howard Broadcasting: CBS Affiliate). Host and coproducer, *In Person,* a monthly hourly television magazine.
Responsibilities included preproduction research, conducting interviews, presenting studio introductions.

June: Marital separation.
Hosted live symphony telecast from Cincinnati Music Hall with Celeste Holm as guest co-host.
Substitute host, *Early Nine Movie.*
Conducted phone-in game show during station

breaks, stumbled with crazy flashing lights and buzzers, and made live jackpot telephone calls.

December: Staff Reporter, Channel 9 News Department. Handled feature and remote news assignments.

1978

January: Spent the coldest month of the worst winter chasing snowplows for updates on road conditions!

February: *In Person* canceled.
Divorce final.

March: Move to Princeton, New Jersey, to accept part-time position in Roger's consulting firm. Contact television and commercial agents to seek opportunities in television. Worry about money and future.
Get Billy settled into new school, make commute to New York for auditions and interviews.

July: Accept offer to co-host *Dialing for Dollars,* WKBW-TV, Buffalo, New York. It was the first solid offer and I grabbed it. Billy off to camp.
Move to Buffalo. Find temporary housing in hotel first month; buy condominium. Fight with movers to get furniture delivered! Learn to be a live talk show co-host!

August: Billy returns from camp. Move into condo. Settle Billy in new school.

September: Change of name and format of *Dialing for Dollars* to *A.M. Buffalo.*
Host new weekly public-affairs show, *Today's Woman* on WKBW-TV.

1979

Contract renewed with WKBW-TV.
Roger calls every night and visits frequently.
Billy blossoms! I enjoy work and new friends.

A.M. Buffalo ratings climb! The highest rated locally produced talk show in nation.
Roger visits every weekend.

1980

March:	Send composite tape to New York talent agency. Fly to New York for meeting with *Today* executive producer. Roger moves to Buffalo!
April:	Accept NBC offer! (And Roger's!) Join *Today Show* as Lifestyle correspondent and commercial spokesperson.
May:	Marry Roger.
June:	Farewell program on *A.M. Buffalo*—two marvelous years! Move to New York.
July:	Present first Lifestyle segment on *Today*. Roger and I have a celebration breakfast!

The list continues with the last four years just as wonderfully jammed with all the things I ever wanted to do, to have, to be, or pursue. And later I will share the important details, the flavors and feelings of those life-changing events, and show how each brought me closer to the goals I have established for myself.

I'm still amazed that a scrawny, straggly-haired girl from the sticks of Nebraska made it to the "big time" world of network television. I actually chatted with Henry Kissinger in the makeup room. Moshe Dayan offered me coffee in the green room before his last *Today* appearance, which was shortly before he died. Liberace let me try on his diamond "piano" ring. Brooke Shields chatted with me about hair spray. Edith Head, though in ill health, made her last television appearance as my guest on *Today*.

I still have to glance at my bulletin board to remind myself that it's all real. There I am at the *Today* anchor desk with Tom Brokaw. There are my interview photos with

Norman Vincent Peale, Donny Osmond, Tom Jones, Jane Fonda, and many other incredible personalities. I have actually interviewed more than two thousand people over the last seven years!

I have continued to be drawn to the high achievers—those who have "made it"—and through the hundreds of hours of interviews and conversations, the thousands of miles of travel, and the special television opportunity to know people I began to hear common themes, methods high achievers had consciously or unconsciously applied to their own success plans. Many of those same themes are the ones that catapulted me into the high-powered, high-paying world of network television. It's true that in the beginning I unwittingly stumbled upon many methods that worked for me, but it wasn't until I came to know the success systems of others that I consciously began to apply them. I have become living proof that they work!

In my efforts to examine and isolate the themes of success I have had the advantage of working in a business that affords me access to the most successful people and to the latest information. The fact that I'm not Jane Pauley or Barbara Walters has actually helped me to reach the real person inside whomever I'm interviewing. There is no reason to fear me, impress me, distrust me, or dislike me. Since my career is still young, people have few preconceived ideas about me. Although it may be easier for a producer to perceive me as a food editor, fashion reporter, weather girl, or movie critic, I am not identified with a given role or specialty, which leaves me free to explore the full range of people and professions, free to probe dreams and ambitions and the "secrets" of success.

The hidden bonus of my work has been the joy I derive from sharing my Lifestyle spots with millions of people. I guess I'm a broadcaster in the true sense, for I love to share the insights I've gained with everyone; it's no fun learning all alone. I have pledged never to abuse the privilege of electronic journalism; whatever I present must be truly informative, enlightening, or entertaining—it must in some way enhance the viewer's day. I vowed never to waste the time of those who

watch my segments. Now, on the threshold of the most rewarding event of my career, writing this book, I repeat that
promise. The chapters that follow are the best of what I have
learned from the experiences of others as well as my own. I
am proud to share these insights and proven principles, and
even prouder to know that they can open up your life to
everything you have ever wanted. You can be bound for
success!

Human growth, the drive to succeed, the search for something better, is truly one of the most exciting aspects of our
existence. Seven years ago, my life was being rained out. By
applying the techniques in this book, I learned to bring out
the sun, to splash a rainbow across the sky, to change the
horizon, to be bound for success!

You can, too!

2

♦

You Gotta Have
a Goal!

Success is the satisfactory
accomplishment of a goal sought for.
—NOAH WEBSTER

THIS BOOK IS all about success—something we are all conscious
of, yet have trouble defining or achieving. We see evidence of
success all around us—expensive automobiles, extravagant
fashions, elegant restaurants, and billboards beckoning us to
travel to exotic lands. We see titles and positions of power in
government and business. We watch glamorous celebrities
whose talent, wealth, and life-styles seem idyllic. They will
tell you that there is satisfaction in acquiring the ornaments
of success, but that those are just a small part of the total,
more complex concept of "success." I prefer Noah Webster's
definition: "Success is the satisfactory accomplishment of a
goal sought for." It's the achievement of a goal that makes
you feel good, gives you a sense of self-worth and purpose.
For someone whose goal is to overcome a lifelong stuttering
problem, delivering a speech before an audience without one
stumble would represent success as much as winning an
Olympic gold medal or getting a major pay raise. For me,
getting a job in television was a goal I sought with great determination.

The people I have observed, interviewed, have known, or studied who are fully successful in every sense of the word are primarily achievers—high achievers, for they are the ones who continue to set new goals, find new boundaries, and exceed their past performances. They seek and enjoy personal growth. These are the individuals who have discovered how to get the most out of their lives and feel good about it. I refer to them as high achievers throughout this book to avoid the misconceptions and physical connotations that accompany the word "successful."

◆ Decide What You Want

In every instance the entrance to a life of true success—a life of growth, achievement, and financial security—begins with a goal: you must decide what you really want! It all begins with that first critical decision.

Jeremy Irons, that handsome actor who won a Tony Award for his Broadway performance in *The Real Thing* and who captivated us in the television series *Brideshead Revisited,* extolled, "I always believed you have to know what you want and you'll get it."

Steve Burzon, the dynamic, high-energy publisher of *Metropolitan Home* magazine, told me, "One day I just decided that I wanted to be a publisher."

Beverly Johnson, the gorgeous top New York fashion model, says that she used to "dream about becoming a model." She looked through some fashion magazines and decided, "If those girls can do it, so can I."

Johnny Carson's zany sidekick, Ed McMahon, decided that he wanted to be an announcer when he was still very young.

Mary Hart, the vivacious co-host of *Entertainment Tonight,* a nationally syndicated television series, started out in Sioux Falls, South Dakota, and she decided what she wanted: "I don't get bogged down by people saying 'No!' I believe if you have a strong enough desire, you can do it. You have to set your mind to achieving your goal."

One hot, sticky evening in Cincinnati I was standing over the stove turning the bacon for an evening meal of bacon, lettuce, and tomato sandwiches. As usual, I was cranky and complained that the boys weren't helping around the house. It seemed that I had been tense, irritable, and dissatisfied for years. In exasperation, my husband asked, "Well, just what is it that you want?" Normally I would have answered something vague, like, "I don't know, but this isn't it," or, "Surely anything is better than this," or, "If I had a little help around here, I might be able to at least find some time to think about it."

On that occasion, however, I took the leap. I had been asking myself that same question: "Just what is it that I really want?" I'd spent a good deal of time searching for an answer. So as my husband waited in angry frustration, I put down the bacon turner and said with uncharacteristic confidence, "First, I want to see what we can do to improve this marriage, and then I want to get a job in television."

That was the moment my life began to change. It wasn't long before we set up an appointment with a marriage counselor, and I began my drive toward landing a job in television. Knowing precisely what you want is the beginning of getting what you want out of life. For some reason, most of us drift through life in ambiguity, tossed from one set of circumstances to another, always waiting to see what will "turn up." The schools I attended never offered a course in the art of setting goals or skills in personal decision making. Yet nothing is more important in determining our future.

I had always assumed that successful people owed their good fortune to "connections"—family money or the "right" education, marriage, or neighborhood. While those special influences can be helpful in and of themselves, they do not assure happiness, success, or fulfillment. In fact, sometimes those "right" connections can rob a person of the drive to discover one's full potential or the satisfaction of achievement. The personal search is postponed forever.

Like most women growing up in the 1950s, I took cues from the women around me, so I learned to please others. It became my mission in life. The message, though indirect, was clear: "The better you please others—parents, husband, children, the church, your teachers—the better you are as a woman." For a woman to set goals for herself, to decide what she wanted for herself, would have been considered selfish and disrespectful; her punishment would be an early death as an old maid.

Far be it from me to disrupt the system! I was an obedient girl and a promising "pleaser." Fortunately, my family impressed me with the need for higher education, and I was among the few graduating high school seniors to attend college. It was simply assumed that I would meet a nice young man and get married. The education should be something practical, like nursing or teaching, something I could fall back on if anything happened to my husband, another big assumption.

One spring afternoon my college adviser surprised me by announcing that it was time to make a firm decision on my major course of study. As a senior faculty member of the University of Nebraska's College of Education, she informed me that there would be excellent opportunities for teachers (if I ever needed to use my teaching degree), and that she had already prepared a draft list of my courses for the following semester. A neat and tidy decision had been made for me, and I was one of the nice little advisees who lined up just like the books lined up on her shelf. Imagine, I didn't even ask for a day or two to think it over!

I did teach high school for a year, but it was a disaster. Since teaching was not my own decision, it set me back several years and added to my personal scrapbook of confusion, guilt, and damaged confidence.

I was not alone, however. Clinical psychologist Harry E. Gunn, a specialist in career counseling, notes that "upward to 60 percent of all Americans say they are not happy with their careers, and that they would rather be in a different field [of work]." Napoleon Hill, author of *Think and Grow Rich,* quotes even higher figures. Hill insists that "ninety-eight out of every hundred people working for wages today are in the positions they hold because they lacked definiteness of decision to plan a definite position."

It is simply a proven fact that in the search for higher achievement, self-improvement, a fuller life, whatever is desired, nothing will change without first *deciding* what you want. There may be an outside chance of a flood, winning a lottery prize, or being discovered by a movie producer who needs your unique face for his epic, but windfall "luck" is a remote possibility, and you can spend a lifetime waiting for divine intervention. My own life did not turn around until I clearly decided what I wanted out of life for myself.

◆ *Mop for Briefcase*

In the 1970s, my life as a homemaker was totally absorbed in car pools, dentist appointments, baseball practice, and dinner parties. But brewing just beneath the surface were ill-defined feelings of frustration, anger, and discontent. Quite predictably, I developed chronic sinus headaches, nagging side effects from the Pill, and a serious kidney infection. I began to think, "This must be it. This must be the way my life will evolve—deteriorating health, days totally consumed by home and family, and a lifetime box seat to sit and watch my husband advance up the corporate ladder." There wasn't much in there for me! I began to watch and wait, brood and throw myself into "projects." Then the realization that some vague outside force was not going to change my life finally began to hit home. I read biographies of successful people in an effort to find clues that might work for me. I attended seminars and workshops on biofeedback and transactional analysis. I took guitar lessons and kept an ear open for part-time work. It took a long time and a good deal of nudging from those seminars and lessons before I realized that I had to take responsibility for my own life. I had to *decide* what I wanted for myself.

It was July 1976 when I put down the bacon turner and declared that I wanted a job in television. On Christmas Eve 1976, the news director of the CBS affiliate in Cincinnati, WCPO-TV, offered me the job as host and co-producer of a new prime-time interview program. Naturally I was thrilled, anxious, apprehensive, but most of all I was astounded at the effectiveness and accuracy of my own goal-setting and goal-attainment methods.

How did I begin my goal setting? I thought carefully about what it would take to make me happy. Did I really want to work? Was I really willing to assume all the demands, responsibilities, and hardships of a full-time job? I longed for greater independence, money of my own, a purpose, an opportunity to learn new skills, new experiences, and the chance to meet and work with professionals. I finally decided that the right job could fulfill those needs.

As I mentally scanned all the jobs that had ever been appealing to me, television kept recurring as the number-one choice. When I definitely settled on the job I wanted, I wrote it down on a slip of paper and kept it with me all the time: "Get a job in television."

◆ Plan and Prepare

With my goal clearly emblazoned on my mind, I began to watch local television with a critical eye. I soon became familiar with the schedules of all three Cincinnati television network affiliates. WCPO-TV, the CBS affiliate, had no woman on any local programming. I discovered that the station was up for their FCC license renewal, a review process mandated every three years. WCPO-TV was my target!

After I had decided which station I wanted to approach, I began to work on the how. I learned the names of the station general manager, the program director, and the news director, who also was the anchor for the station's top-rated evening newscasts. The news director was a local legend, a tough newspaper journalist who made a successful transition first into radio and later into television. A no-nonsense, no-fluff newsman.

I worked on my resume, listing all my previous work experience, including my part-time work. My husband's secretary typed the final draft for me and made a dozen copies. I was finally in business for real.

It was time to set a date for my first visit to WCPO-TV. Jeff and Bill would be in school a full day beginning in September, so I set my WCPO-TV date for mid-October and I wrote it on the calendar. I made daily menu charts, hired regular cleaning help, and found new ways to cut down on my chauffeuring duties. Meanwhile, I read all the local newspaper columns on television, picked up magazines with information on television programming and personalities, and began to read magazines for working women.

◆ Work on the Outside

I collected as much as I could on the television business, but I knew that I needed further preparation. I needed to feel comfortable in the role of a working mother, a job applicant, a professional. But I wasn't any of those things yet, so how could I feel that I was functioning in a role I had yet to attain? How could I apply for a job with the confidence of a seasoned professional with dog hairs on my skirt and peanut butter under my nails?

My wardrobe could be grouped into three categories: at-home grubbies, party dresses, and PTA dresses (only two). I had nothing appropriate for an interview, and I'd be in real trouble if I had to begin dressing for work five days a week! I dipped into my allowance and bought a basic gray flannel suit with gray pumps, three blouses, and a beginner's briefcase. I just wasn't ready for the real thing—that was going too far. So I bought an envelope-type folio in tan suede. Even though it was flat, with effort I could squeeze in a can of hair spray, a hairbrush, extra panty hose, and, of course, my dozen resumes. I wore the new gray outfit several times so I would feel at home in it, and I practiced using the folio instead of a purse until it felt as natural as my old shoulder bag.

◆ Work on the Inside

I had yet to learn about the powers of visualization, but instinctively it felt good to think about myself wearing business clothes, carrying a real briefcase, walking, talking, relating to people as a professional. I imagined myself sitting behind a desk, answering the phone, dealing with other professionals with ease. As I learned more about the television business, as I read about the problems and rewards of working mothers, as I visualized myself in the role of a professional, I grew more comfortable and confident, and more sure that what I was doing was right for me. All the time my goal remained as strong as a beacon, guiding my actions and sustaining my determination. In the chapter on visualization, you will learn how to visualize and stimulate your own goals.

♦ *Get Started!*

When the day of my visit to WCPO-TV arrived, I was full of positive anticipation and enthusiasm, and I was scared to death. Driving into the city, I was holding a private pep rally, so by the time I arrived at the station I felt like the little engine that could—"I think I can, I think I can, I know I can! . . ." It must have worked, because I breezed into the employee entrance like a veteran. I took note of the receptionist's nameplate, greeted her by name as I introduced myself, and asked to see Mr. Hevel, the program manager. Miraculously she replied, "You're in luck. He just returned from vacation and you can go right on up."

That was the great beginning of what would have been the bitter end of an imagined career. Mr. Hevel was cordial, took my resume, and patiently explained that while there were no jobs open, there might be some commercial work. He set up an interview with the commercial production manager for the following week.

I trekked in the next week to discover that there was only an occasional need for a female commercial spokesperson. For the most part station talent handled those extra chores. However, he assured me that he would be sure to call "should anything turn up."

I had set a goal. I had made a commitment to it. I felt it pulsing in my veins. I had gotten this far on nothing but desire. I would get the rest of the way.

It was obvious that the commercial production manager had signed off with me. He began stacking papers on his cluttered desk, giving me that "your time is up" look, when I calmly insisted that I was willing to take any job at the station to get started, but it had to be full-time. By this time he was getting impatient. His secretary announced that he had a long-distance telephone call holding; as he picked up the phone and turned away, he said, "Look, that's about all I can do for you. Why don't you talk to Al Sherman [name changed], the news director-legend, about something in his department?" That was all I needed to keep my goal burning.

◆ *Keep the Goal Burning*

As I felt the office of the commercial production manager, feeling somewhat discouraged and confused about my next steps, who should walk out of the studio but Al Sherman himself! I fell in step behind him all the way into his office. I couldn't believe I was so bold; goals give you a special bravado! I introduced myself, added that our entire family loved his news programs, and mentioned several recent segments that I'd found informative.

Al Sherman, however, was true to his reputation as a tough, hard-nosed, serious journalist. He was unmoved by my enthusiasm and unimpressed with my resume. He quickly pointed out that I had no journalism background and probably no grasp of the realities of the business. News was certainly not the slick, glamorous world of entertainment! There were wars to cover, urban squalor, local government corruption, city politics, and road conditions. Perhaps I should go back to my family and be thankful that I had such a comfortable life.

My goal burned brightly, along with a deep indignation at the suggestion that I somehow wasn't cut out for the work. I insisted that I could learn what I didn't know and said I wasn't afraid of hard work. I then quietly reminded him that WCPO was the only station in the market that did not employ a woman as on-air talent. The room became deadly silent. Then Sherman's stony face cracked into a sly grin as he said, "Fine, perhaps we can set up an audition."

◆ *Give It Your Best*

Before I fully realized what had happened, Sherman began to outline the audition requirements.

"Maybe you'd better write this down. First, I want you to write two original reports, each about three minutes long. One should be a hard-news story, the other is to be lighter, more human interest in nature. Then I want you to prepare a four-minute newscast from wire copy. In addition, I want you to conduct an interview with a juvenile-court judge. We'll get some fresh wire copy for you to take along with you. Now, can you come in tomorrow night to do this?"

I was too stunned for words, but when he said "tomorrow night" I came to my senses fast. There was no way I could prepare such an audition for the following night. After checking studio availability, Sherman decided that I could come in on Thursday, four days away. Only four days to write two reports, a newscast, and an interview with a guest on a subject about which I knew nothing!

To this day I believe that the audition was a legitimate attempt to get Nancy Foreman out of the hallways of WCPO-TV forever. I doubt if Al Sherman expected to see me again. But I had a goal I was determined to reach.

All the way home from WCPO-TV my knees shook; I was alternately elated and terrified; I felt hot, then cold. My mind raced; I replayed the entire scene in my head, then frantically began spinning ideas for the reports. I would have to start immediately! When I got home I went to bed instead. Dinner didn't matter.

The next day I unrolled the yards of wire copy all over the living room floor. I had never seen wire copy before. Some of the type was so faint I could hardly read it, and there were dozens and dozens of news stories. Which one should I choose? What about the reports; what should they be about? Interview a juvenile-court judge! They can't be serious.

First I tackled the newscast. With a scissors I cut the most interesting stories apart and arranged them under headings: international, national, local. Then I began to eliminate. I read them aloud to get a rough idea of the time and kept eliminating until I got them down to three and a half minutes. I began to rewrite the stories so they would read smoothly, then wrote the connecting transitions. It took the entire first day to write one-fourth of the audition! And I hadn't even begun to rehearse it.

The next day, I combed the newspapers and latest issues of *Time* and *Newsweek*. I found a hard-core news story with several difficult foreign names that I would master, and I went to work. The softer report was more fun. Since it would soon be the Christmas season I decided to report on the fragrance business. The trick was to show my personality without being flip and to include my own observations and experience as well as industry data and trends.

The interview was much tougher, and I was running out of time. After digging up a few articles on teenage crime, I wrote down all the things I wanted to know about juvenile problems, the legal process for youth, correction facilities, and the role of the courts vs. the role of parents. After arranging all the information in sequence, I wrote questions that would elicit the information I wanted. It was like writing a report backward!

I saved an entire day for rehearsal and getting comfortable in my new role as a television professional. Sitting on the edge of the bed, I read the newscast to the sweep hand of the clock radio. I wanted the timing to be perfect—a pause here, speeding up there, could make the difference. I practiced reading to the mirror, then to our family camera. I asked my list of questions to an imaginary guest, silently answering each one.

This was my opportunity of a lifetime. I may not get a job, but if I failed to do the required work, I was *guaranteed* not to get it. I worked as hard as I had ever worked, all the while continuing to manage the family.

The day of the audition I felt like all my nerve endings were standing up to be counted. I arrived at the studio early in hopes that I would have an opportunity to get familiar with the studio surroundings. Instead, I was shown to a vacant office where I waited and waited. I would have preferred waiting for the dentist. My stomach threatened to revolt, but I drank tea and humored myself: "Sure would be swell, Nance, if you blew your big chance by throwing up on your audition!"

The chilly studio was cavernous, dark, and smelled of hot electric wiring. The guys on the floor routinely positioned the chair, untangled the cord for a mike, and without ceremony asked me to have a seat. We would be ready shortly. The tension of the moment or my adrenalin level overcame my nausea, and without much warning I was getting the countdown from the floor director.

I heard myself start on cue, and as I progressed through

the newscast I felt as if I were watching myself from a dark corner of the studio. My voice, though steady, sounded thin and shallow. But I gathered confidence as I continued to read. There was a brief break after the reports while a second chair was added for my interview with the juvenile-court judge. His answers to my questions were close to the ones I had rehearsed (for the guest), and at the end I thanked the guest, signed off, and asked the "viewers" to join me again the next day—just like a pro! When it was over, and the lights dimmed, I was jubilant. I didn't have to stop and start over, there had been only one minor stumble, and I didn't even throw up! I expected applause, congratulations, or even just "Nice job." Instead, they all seemed to go casually about their business.

I was told that Al Sherman would probably give me a call when he returned from vacation. I left the chilly studio dazed, exhausted, and famished.

The six weeks of waiting that followed were agony. I was almost ready to chalk up the audition to "experience," when Al Sherman himself called to tell me that the news department was developing a new prime-time interview show, and *I was to be the host!*

I gave it my best, and it paid off! These techniques can pay off for you, too.

It all begins with a goal, a deeply felt, passionate desire. Maxwell Maltz, author of *Psycho-Cybernetics,* notes, "Man (and woman) is by nature a goal-striving being. And because he is built that way he is not happy unless he is functioning as he was made to function—as a goal striver." As Dr. Maltz states, we are simply following our true natures when we set goals. In *Think and Grow Rich,* Napoleon Hill flatly declares, "There is one quality which one must possess to win, and that is *definiteness of purpose,* the knowledge of what one wants, and a burning *desire* to possess it."

I was all too familiar with the propaganda: "Know thyself," "To thine own self be true." But life certainly sends out conflicting, mixed-up signals. Like so many others, I had neglected my true needs. As Dr. Iris Sangiuliano, author of *In Her Time,* says, "By and large we [women] are late bloomers; we postpone ourselves." Not only had I failed to set clear goals for my own life, I had denied the need, too. Since we are not taught to give ourselves permission to explore our deepest needs and priorities, it seems uncomfortable and self-indulgent to start thinking about ourselves.

◆ Go Soul-Searching

We must nurture our own needs, goals, and aspirations before we can be truly successful, happy, fulfilled and before we can be fully capable of relating to others—even our spouse, our children, or our parents. Remember, we are goal strivers by nature. We must find and appreciate our inner needs. We must nurture and express them, find ways of translating them into solid accomplishments.

David Seabury discovered this truth in 1937. In *The Art of Selfishness,* he writes:

> Everything that lives, from the moment it comes into being, seeks its nourishment and continues so to seek. The food of man is emotional and mental as well as physical. He who does not ask, even demand, his right to special nourishment sickens and becomes a burden. . . . Your duty is to yourself.

Learn what you really want out of life. Do some soul-searching; really think about your goals. It is hard work, uncomfortable work, but don't underestimate the significance of this first and most important step in becoming successful. You deserve to get what you want out of life. You are by nature a goal-seeking being. You have mental and emotional needs that are as important to your existence as food. Don't deny or avoid these realities. Don't feel guilty or apologetic for seeking a better life, for growing or achieving beyond others, even beyond yourself.

Be prepared to spend extra time deciding on your goals. We have become conditioned to make instant, sometimes impulsive decisions—what to buy, where to go, what to wear. The big decisions of our lives, like what we really want, can't be rushed. Plan to spend time each day soul-searching—thinking about all the things you would like to do, to have, to be, to become. It usually takes several weeks of difficult probing to actually complete a working list of goals. During this time you may have some strange dreams or rather unsettling ideas, even some sleepless nights. Your mind is working overtime on a project that is of the greatest importance to you. Let it happen!

◆ Go Soaring

Let your imagination soar! Begin by thinking of the most outrageous, delicious things and experiences. Command your own private Lear jet. Lounge on the deck of your private yacht. See the title of "President" on your office door as you walk into your custom-furnished corner office with its sweeping vista of the nation's largest city. Your mind has no limits. Arrive at your villa in Spain or your ski chalet in Switzerland by private train.

For most people this is a strange new exercise, because from the time we are children our options are limited. Modern child psychology teaches parents and teachers to present limited choices: "These are the three movies we can consider. Which one would you like to see?" "Which of these two shirts would you like to wear today?" "Your score on the aptitude tests indicates that you should consider a career in accounting or teaching." Sound familiar? No wonder we grow up looking to others for alternatives. We grow up with limited options. Then we limit ourselves. Now is the time to remove the limits, lift the boundaries, and have fun! It's a great exercise!

As your mental soaring settles into more realistic modes, think about what you want among all those possibilities. Ask yourself:

1. What do I want to know?
2. What do I want to do?
3. What do I want out of a relationship?
4. How do I want to spend my time?
5. What do I want to own?

Begin a working list of goals. Write them all down. It doesn't matter that some seem impossible or trivial or selfish. Consider it a first draft. Get it all on paper!

◆ Watch Out!

As you develop your list of goals there are several pitfalls to watch for:

1. Don't set any goals for yourself that involve others. Don't decide that you want the best marriage in America because that requires the efforts of two people. Don't decide that your son will become a doctor because that establishes a goal for someone else, which is one of the most popular avoidance maneuvers. Parents set goals for their children and mistakenly believe that they will derive as much vicarious satisfaction. Meanwhile the child is burdened with a goal that isn't his own. Your goals must be for yourself.

2. Don't hang on to wrong or outdated goals of the past. Unfortunately, most of us feel a strong obligation to carry out choices that may be all wrong for us. Although I dreaded teaching, I felt that I should use my degree and follow through on a choice that really wasn't my own to begin with. We are taught to "finish what we start" or "stick with our choice no matter what." Too often we feel that we have to make it work, whether it's a bad marriage or a car that's a lemon. Recognize your wrong decisions and disconnect them. Cut your loss and move on.

3. Don't accept your first list of goals as final. For most of us, our prior conditioning is so strong that the first goals that pop into our heads are the automatic responses that have been deeply embedded in our subconscious, rather than the honest answers to the question "What do I really want out of life?" Since we seldom take the time for this kind of honest soul-searching, the temptation is to take the easy course and list activities that are already under way—a kind of "jobs to be completed" list. Setting goals that reflect your personal needs, skills, and talents is a very difficult task. Psychiatrists make a lot of money listening to frustrated patients trying to work out the problem of what they really want for themselves. Chances are you don't need a career counselor or an analyst.

You can do it for yourself, but it does take effort. Don't give up in frustration. Keep your concentration tuned to your working list of goals!

4. Don't underestimate your potential. And don't overestimate your potential. You are working toward a final set of goals that will be challenging, but not impossible; that will stretch you to new heights, but will be reachable. Don't decide that you want to have three million dollars tomorrow (unless you plan to rob a bank). On the other hand, don't set a goal that's too easy. Don't decide that you want to write a book if you have already written three. Set realistic goals, but make them *goals*—something to strive for, something that pushes you beyond your present limits.

5. Carry your list of goals with you in your wallet or purse, and look at it several times a day. Think about how it would feel to have attained those goals. Some won't stand up to the test. Eliminate some; add others. Rearrange according to priority. Work with the list, and watch it gradually take shape.

◆ The Turning Point

Many of us reach a level of growth that forces us to take stock of our lives and review our priorities. I was frustrated, miserable, and hopeless when I reached the important turning point in my life. I had to make some tough decisions in order to change my life for the better. Perhaps you have felt the constriction of the present and the restless need to grow. Even the legendary success authority himself, Dale Carnegie, started out miserably and faced the desperate need to change. He lived in a shabby, roach-infested room in New York while he worked as a truck salesman, a job he loathed. He writes:

> I knew I had everything to gain and nothing to lose by giving up the job I despised. I wasn't interested in making a lot of money, but I was interested in making a lot of living. In short, I had come to the Rubicon—that moment of decision—that decision completely altered my future.

It not only altered his future; it enriched the lives of millions.

◆ Be a Goal Buster!

You have gone through several lists of goals. You've had good days and bad days agonizing over the things you really want. You have gone soaring with your imagination and tried on all the possibilities and possessions you could dream up. You have accepted any limitations that would be unwise and unnecessary to try to overcome. Instead, you have found exciting *realistic* goals that meet your deepest needs while being consistent with your special skills, talents, and potentials. Now it's time to form your final set of goals. This becomes a powerful, binding contract with yourself. It is the beginning—the contract for higher achievement, new friends, more money, new skills, more time for hobbies or family—just about whatever you have always wanted.

Don't think for a moment that you can skip this important step. Just as a legal contract confirms a transaction, the process of writing your goals according to a specific form reinforces your commitment and starts the wheels of change. It works!

1. Divide a large sheet of paper into thirds, and write these categories: Work, Relationships, Wealth.

2. Under each of the three categories write Short-Term and Long-Term.

3. Select no more than four or five goals for each category: two under Short-Term, and two or three under Long-Term.

GOAL CONTRACT

WORK:
    —Short-Term
    1. My goal is to win the Acme account.
    2. My goal is:
    —Long-Term
    1. My goal is to operate my own advertising agency.
    2. My goal is:

RELATIONSHIPS:
  —Short-Term
  1. My goal is to find a friend who likes French gourmet cooking.
  2. My goal is:
  —Long-Term
  1. My goal is to attract a man (woman) who will harmonize with my needs and share my growth.
  2. My goal is:

WEALTH:
  —Short-Term
  1. My goal is to own a hot tub.
  2. My goal is:
  —Long-Term
  1. My goal is to build a retirement portfolio of tax-deferred bonds and securities.
  2. My goal is:

Understand that those are the goals that you really want and are prepared to spend years, if need be, to achieve. This list is a powerful contract with yourself.

◆ *Stay on Track!*

To keep myself on track, I draw my goal chart in vivid colors on oversized newsprint paper and tape it on my closet door so it's the first thing I see when I wake up in the morning. Many people keep a goal notebook which includes all their earlier drafts of goals—those that didn't make the final cut. I like to carry a copy of the goals in my wallet calendar. That way, I can easily pull it out to look at during the day. It's amazing how a look at my goals gives me a lift when I feel tired or discouraged.

Several people I talked to taped their goals to the bathroom mirror and read them aloud the first thing in the morning. Try repeating them to music during your shower. Try changing locations frequently so they don't become part of the scenery. Try writing the three categories on different colored paper, then tuck them in places where you will find them at odd times—like in your favorite beaded purse, taped to a Christmas tie, or stuck in your phone book under "Z."

The other day I drove into the parking lot of our local post office. As I got out of the car I noticed that the dashboard of the car next to mine was covered with three-by-five cards filled with goal statements: "You are the most important person!" "Make it happen today," and "Take time to imagine." Over the glove compartment hung a carefully written list of personal goals, beginning with "Lose 15 pounds" and "Read one hour a day" and ending with "Buy a new car with this year's commissions!" Now there's a man who's developed his own system!

Be creative! Try out different ways of keeping your goals in mind. Integrate them into your daily life, and you will be surprised how quickly they become part of your conscious and unconscious efforts. Once you decide what you really want, and commit yourself to attaining those goals, nothing will stop you from getting what you want!

◆◆◆

- Decide what you want for yourself. Explore your deepest desires.
- Exercise your imagination—overcome past conditioning and "limited options."
- Write down all your goals on paper as they come to mind.
- Consider your existing talents, skills, and liabilities.
- Work and live with the list—eliminate some goals, add others, and arrange them according to priority.
- Develop a realistic but challenging goal contract, following the directions and example.
- Make your goal reminders that you carry with you and extras that you place strategically in your living and working spaces.

◆◆◆

Congratulations! You have just completed one of the toughest and most important steps toward higher achievement and a richer life.

3

◆

On the Goal Road

*There is nothing paltry about
the man (or woman) who is struggling,
not to be great or to hobnob with the great,
but to be greater than he (or she) is.*

—"Graduating Into Life"
Royal Bank of Canada monthly letter

Now THAT YOU'VE drawn up your goal contract and it's in your wallet or on your wall, you are ready to begin bringing those goals into reality. Be aware, however, that you may encounter a number of delays, detours, and washouts along the goal road. The first thing I had to learn was to give myself permission. I had to overcome a lifetime of seeking permission to get what I wanted. I had to tell myself that it was okay to want a job, even though we could manage without the extra salary. I had to give myself permission to spend money on career clothes. I had to grant myself permission to cut down on time spent driving kids all over Hamilton and Warren counties. The family could work together to figure out how to get where they wanted to go. Someone like me, who had grown up trying to please others, will have an especially tough time with this one. I had to give myself permission to set goals for myself!

◆ *Give Yourself Permission*

Learn to give yourself permission to decide on goals for yourself without consulting anyone else. Give yourself permission to achieve them, to be successful. Give yourself permission to be happy and to get what you want out of life. It's a perfectly acceptable part of growing up. That's the rub, however.

Early on we learn that good little boys and girls ask permission to play with a friend, leave the table after a meal, cross the street, buy candy, go steady, marry. At school we have to ask permission to speak, check out a book, go on a field trip, even go to the bathroom! As children we learn our lessons well, for survival, approval, acceptance. We are constantly rewarded for asking permission and proceeding only if it is granted. And if we fail to get the necessary permissions, we are punished. It's understandable how those lessons become an integral part of our decision-making process. When we have become "programmed" to need permission for our major, and in some cases minor, decisions, the ordeal of making an independent decision can be wrenching. The permission-dependent person is constantly looking for permission from a parent, sibling, boss, relative, or friend, and it's a tough habit to break.

Why has it become a habit? Why does the need for permission linger on into adulthood? Psychologists tell us that as children we found acceptance and approval through obediently asking for permission, and that felt good. We were rewarded and patted on the head. As adults we want to continue to be accepted and to get the approval of others, so unconsciously we continue to use behavior that we know worked in the past, even though it no longer applies.

Another potent force than can discourage us from granting ourselves permission is fear. Like smoke, it weaves thin vapors of vague, ominous feelings that say, "Uh-oh, I don't know about that. It's different, new, could be dangerous . . . could be uncomfortable . . . could be risky . . . could be a lot of work. . . . Better keep things the way they are." If you were to press for reasons and ask, "What is it that makes you afraid to give yourself permission?" most people wouldn't know the answer. I have pressed and was told, "Well, I don't know exactly." Sometimes people are afraid they will regret spending the money; sometimes they are afraid of making a mistake or are uneasy about trying something new. One of the big fears is the guilt that may follow.

◆ Permission Without Guilt

One wise mother wrote to psychologist Dr. Martha Friedman, "When we had children we bought a home in order to give them roots. But when they became old enough we gave them wings." Sadly, few parents understand that the most generous gift that could be given to children is the ability to make their own decisions, without a lifetime of needing parental (or any other) permission.

When psychologist Dr. David Seabury decided to continue his studies abroad, he received letters from eight of his mother's friends. All reminded him that his mother was sixty-two, and each unfolded her own brand of guilt, calling him irresponsible, selfish, and other uglies. He remained firm in his decision to leave home, and before his mother died at ninety-two, she told him how glad she was that he had continued his education in Europe, for if he had interrupted his work for thirty years on her account, their relationship would have been severely damaged. He was a very courageous and farsighted young man to have stuck by such an important decision in the face of powerful opposition.

If we are to achieve our goals, if we are to improve and grow and move our lives toward those things in life that we really want, we must learn to give ourselves no-guilt permission. If I had waited for permission to break out of my discontent and depression, I would still be in that house in Ohio staining the woodwork and ordering gravel for the mudholes in the driveway.

◆ Permission Granted

Permission dependency no longer has to keep you from your goals. It no longer has to hold you back, retard your growth. It is a habit that can be changed.

Start small and work up to the larger decisions. The next time you find yourself agonizing over a small decision like which blouse to buy, whether to order the fish or the veal, whether to paint the porch white or yellow, stop and ask yourself why you're spending such a disproportionate amount of time on such an insignificant decision. What are you waiting for? Mother's approval? Daddy's? Hubby's, or wifey's? Who's in charge here? Who is going to wear the blouse and eat the veal? Whose needs are you meeting? Give yourself permission! And don't fuss over the one you didn't choose. If you hear yourself moaning about how you should have ordered fish or should have taken the green blouse, you are really undermining your independence.

Make those important decisions on your own, without permission from anyone. It gets easier and you gradually become more confident. If the fish is lousy, and the veal looks delicious—so what? It probably won't be the last meal you'll ever eat. Next time you will probably avoid the fish in that restaurant. If you're disappointed with the white paint on the porch, big deal. Paint over it. These are not mistakes; they are trials. Even the trials feel good when they are your own.

The smaller decisions become easier, and you will gradually stop looking and waiting for outside permission. You will soon begin to give yourself permission to make the larger decisions. Will you spend your vacation with relatives or take a cruise with a friend? Which job offer will you accept? Which car is right for you? Go ahead and look for sound advice that may help you make better, more informed choices. It's important to be open to information and the experience of others—but make your own decisions. You do not have to ask permission or seek approval from anyone.

◆◆

- Give yourself permission to set goals for yourself.
- Give yourself permission to achieve them.
- After doing your homework and listening to sound advice from others, make your own decisions.
- Give yourself permission to make an occasional wrong decision. We can all learn from "trials."
- Refuse to feel any guilt if your decision is right for you.
- Give yourself permission to be happy!

◆◆

◆ Be a Learner—Sign Up!

New information, continued learning, new experiences, and ideas all come together on the goal road. High achievers are also higher-learning consumers. Many found that special learning experiences have brought them closer to their goals. Some actively sign up for specialized programs; others just stumble into really life-changing experiences. I had to be pushed, but fortunately my important learning experience pushed me into a better, more independent life.

In July 1976, a friend of mine called to invite me to join a group that would be attending a seminar on transactional analysis. Her husband was chairman of the Institute of Business and Community Relations at Xavier University in Cincinnati; he would be conducting the weekend workshop. It seemed that a couple of people had dropped out, and they needed someone who could "sit in" as a guest. As she explained to me, companies select certain employees to attend T.A. seminars in an effort to help them get their careers back on track or to improve management or personnel problems. The tuition was hefty, more than I would ever spend on such an experience for myself. I stalled. The thought of spending a long weekend sitting in a steamy college classroom during one of Cincinnati's hottest Julys didn't seem very appealing. But Marilyn coaxed me into giving it a try. That weekend experience changed my whole outlook on life.

At the time I was thirty-five. My husband was a hardworking middle-management executive in a large corporation. Our two sons were eleven and seven. We owned a big new home on seven acres outside Cincinnati. I was miserable! I had everything that society promised would make me happy; instead I felt unfulfilled and cheated.

I came to the T.A. seminar a reluctant observer. I was soon surprised to discover how hungry I was for information that could improve my life, for a way to figure out what I was feeling and why, and to discover that there were still options open for me.

We learned about setting goals, about self-defeating behavior, about taking control of our lives and making decisions. I learned that the responsibility for my life didn't have to be left to destiny or fate. I had to take control, or others would, and by not making a decision I was really making a decision. That is, by sitting back and not asserting my right to make my own decisions, I was abdicating much of my own life. Most of the time I didn't recognize the decisions that were mine to make. Although it may have been unconscious, I was actually deciding to be passive, to avoid independent decision making. It was all new material to me, and pretty heady at that. We also learned not to wait for permission from the outside; we could give ourselves permission to go ahead with a decision and avoid self-defeating behavior that sometimes sabotages our own progress.

Sara Eyestone is another example of someone whose life was changed through a group program. You may recognize the name. Sara Eyestone is one of the nation's foremost batik artists. Sara dropped out of college to get married and start a family. She didn't pick up a paintbrush until she was thirty-one and had four children and an ailing marriage. She started a nursery school, designed jewelry, became an artist's model, and went through the tunnels of self-doubt. But it was Overeaters Anonymous that gave her the push she needed to begin making decisions that would change her life. "I learned that I couldn't change anybody but myself. I learned to take control of my life, my body, my emotions. . . . You're the only one who can make yourself happy. We can't expect anyone else to make us happy. We have to learn how."

Sara went to Overeaters Anonymous with a friend, hoping to lose weight, but what she learned gave her far more than weight loss.

Currently there is an explosion of self-help programs which some believe to be a collective search for growth and improvement, for control over our lives. If you need a boost to get your systems working or the reinforcement that a group dynamic can provide, look for a short-term program that matches your personality and style. For me it was T.A.; for Sara Eyestone it was Overeaters Anonymous. But be careful of the self-help trap. Our media-inflicted society often promotes these self-help programs as panaceas instead of the guides they really are—you have to do the tough "inside" work for yourself. Don't expect the program to do the work, and don't settle for the superficial change and the latest self-help jargon just to impress others.

One of the most dynamic men I have interviewed is Ateo Gulino, former president of Dubois International, a huge chemical company based in Cincinnati. Mr. Gulino is the son of a tailor who worked his way to the top. Gulino travels all over the world, is under enormous pressure, maintains two homes, and obviously isn't the type to sign up for a night course in hatha yoga for beginners, but his commitment to continued learning requires remarkable discipline.

Each year Gulino selects one subject that interests him. Every book he reads, his leisure travel, his television viewing, and his entertainment are directed toward increasing his knowledge of that one subject. He finds experts in his subject and corresponds with them. He develops reading lists and finds lectures on the subject. Consequently, at the end of each year he becomes a virtual expert himself. Over the years his studies have included World War II, the Vikings, and Shakespeare.

While I admire Mr. Gulino's commitment to learning and his year-long discipline, I don't have the attention span for that kind of in-depth study. My work requires mental speed-shifting in a wide range of subjects. However, I do know that an enormous amount of time is wasted on irrelevant reading and television viewing. The number of magazines, newspapers, and trash novels that glut the market and our mailboxes is mind-boggling. Yet only a few are really necessary to stay well informed. If you track the feature stories of the major consumer news magazines over a period of years, as I have, you'll find that the same information is continually recycled. How many times do you have to read about cellulite, office romances, the hazards of jogging, the dangers of caffeine, what it's like to be Cathy Lee Crosby . . . Shall I go on?

After you have decided on your goals, read selectively. Choose carefully the television programs you watch. Don't waste time on junk information! Soon you'll find that your reading, television viewing, even your conversations will be more focused on your goals. It's a natural result of keeping your goals clearly in mind and having a willingness, an eagerness to learn. As you become a more discriminating information consumer, this selective process will gradually become automatic, leaving you more time to spend on constructive activity directed toward achieving your goals.

◆◆

- Sign up for seminars that will help you overcome impediments that are holding you back.
- Search out continuing education programs that can lead you to your goals.
- Monitor your reading, television viewing, and telephone conversations to avoid wasting your time and mental resources.

◆◆

◆ Accept the Challenge

As a child I was told that I was not athletic: "Nancy is so feminine. She doesn't like sports—they're too rough." I bought that story for a while, but the truth was that our small-town school didn't have a regular sports program, so there was no way to know what I could do. I was thirty-one when my husband decided that we should learn to ski. I was frightened and apprehensive. The first day was a nightmare. I was tense, self-conscious, and inhibited. At the end of the day the instructor announced that we would learn to use the pomalift the next morning. Then he looked right at me, curled his lips, and said, "I know which little snow bunny is going to have the most trouble."

It was the nicest thing he could have done for me. The "red flare" went up. The "red flare" is my private alert system that signals a challenge. Like a smoke alarm, the red flare leads me to the source, helps me define the challenge, and pushes me to take the necessary action. The instructor's sarcastic remark sent up the "red flare," and I decided then and there that I was going to use that pomalift as if I'd been born on it! The lifts opened at 8:00 A.M.; our classes started at 9:00. For an hour I went up and down the beginner's slope on the pomalift. I fell off, picked myself up, and asked the lift operator for suggestions. I just kept at it. I held the sneering face of the instructor in my mind; it kept the "red flare" going. I wanted to prove that I could make it, not just to him, but to myself. When I joined the class at 9:00 A.M. for the first ride on the pomalift, I handled it with ease while several of the star pupils from the day before fell off. By the end of the week I was one of the best skiers in the class. Believe me, nothing could have brought me more satisfaction than that personal victory.

As you pursue your goals, be prepared to meet challenges from the inside, the outside, and sometimes from both at the same time. My "red flare" goes off when I need to prove something. With it comes a little anger and curiosity. Anger, in some cases, because someone isn't giving me credit for something I know I can do or know I can learn to do. Curiosity, because I would really like to find out myself just how I measure up to the test. It's probably similar to the drive that athletes feel when they set out to break a record—either their own or someone else's.

The "red flare" goes off whenever anyone decides that I cannot do something without first letting me try. My red flare went up when Al Sherman at WCPO-TV decided that I wasn't the news type, and then again when he loaded me with an unreasonable audition and suggested that I present it the next night. In the case of the ski lifts, it was over thirty years before I could disprove the judgment others had made concerning my untested abilities.

OUTSIDE CHALLENGES

Some challenges blow up like a storm. Others begin as a simple, whimsical desire.

Lore Caulfield was an independent film producer in Los Angeles. In 1974, after she had completed an important television documentary, she decided on a little reward for herself—something special, something she had always wanted: pure silk bikini panties. She couldn't find any. As she continued to search, even calling stores across the country, she became more determined that she would have her silk panties. The red flare went up and it became a challenge. The fact that they weren't available made her even more adamant. She bought a bolt of silk and employed a dressmaker to help her design a pair of perfect-fitting panties. She had the entire bolt made into bikini panties. When she showed them to friends at the office, it seemed everyone wanted to buy them. They were such a hit that she took a pair to the lingerie buyer at Robinson's Department Store, who immediately ordered twenty dozen of her bikinis to retail at twenty dollars a pair. Today, Lore Lingerie is a multimillion-dollar business—Lore designs are featured in the wardrobes of Linda Evans and Joan Collins on *Dynasty,* and are worn by millions of American women.

INSIDE CHALLENGES

Most people have their hands full dealing with smaller, day-to-day challenges, but high achievers tend to go looking for challenges, and if they can't find the right one, they set up their own! Pam Reising, a truly remarkable woman, appeared as my guest on *Today* as an expert on antique quilts. She is also sales manager of consumer products for Sterns and Foster Company, which is based in Cincinnati. That alone is a demanding job, but in addition she turned her hobby into a lucrative business. Pam opened a quilt shop in Cincinnati and began selling quilting supplies and giving lessons. Her expertise in antique quilts also makes her a popular guest speaker and consultant. As we sipped coffee in the green room waiting to do our spot on quilts, Pam told me about a challenge she carefully selected for herself in an effort to promote her own confidence and growth. Her story makes my hair stand on end!

Pam said that she wanted a "personal test to find my limits physically and mentally." She also thought of herself as physically weak, and laughingly mentioned that she couldn't open a jar of peanut butter or raise a sticky window. So she signed up for a week with Outward Bound, a program that specializes in camping and survival experiences for adults. Her group would go mountain climbing in the heart of the Rocky Mountains. Every ounce of her strength, stamina, endurance, and raw nerve would be tested. For three months prior to her departure, Pam went to a gym for rigorous daily workouts to increase her strength and to build up her upper body. "My body will never be the same," she proudly told me. "I always had very narrow shoulders; now they're much broader and more athletic."

Her challenge was even more harrowing than she had hoped and feared. Since Pam had spent most of her life on land in the Midwest, it didn't occur to her that she might not like the feeling of heights. She counted on having some fears, but not the fear of heights. However, Pam managed her acrophobia, along with the other hardships and physical discomforts, and made it to the summit. There was only one other member of the team who made it to the top with Pam!

"Would you do it again?" I asked.

"I don't have to," she confidently replied. "What I needed to prove, I proved. But let me tell you . . . that experience changed my life. Now when I confront a task that at first seems impossible, I know that I can do it. I made it to the top of that mountain, and that experience has become a part of who I am. I have a much better perspective on life; petty matters no longer seem important. And I have gained a deep confidence that no outside circumstances can take away."

Pam Reising accepted the challenge of her own physical limitations, her feelings of inadequacy, and her fear of heights, then conquered them all when she reached the top of that mountain. She signed up for an experience that would teach her to overcome those inner frailties that had been holding her back. Even though her family and friends discouraged her from going, Pam gave herself permission to go after what was important to her own growth. And what's more, she gave herself permission to succeed!

◆◆◆

- Challenges present special opportunities for growth and achievement. Whenever you hear anyone telling you that something you want to do is impossible or "highly unlikely," or can't be done because others have failed at it— send up your "red flare." Remember, no one but you can determine what you can do.
- Accept your personal challenges of undeveloped or untested abilities. Is there a ski slope or mountaintop that will help you overcome your limitations and find new confidence? Meet your challenges head on with an adventurous spirit and anticipate new heights of achievement!

◆◆◆

4

♦

Visualization

Imagination rules the world.

—NAPOLEON

*The faculty of imagination is the great
spring of human activity and the principal
source of human improvement.*

—DUGALD STEWART
Scottish philosopher

IF I HAD to choose what I considered the most important chapter of the book, it would be this one. Visualization is an ability we all have, but few realize what a powerful tool it can be when applied to a specific plan of achievement.

Our minds possess enormous powers that we seldom use. "The imagination is literally the workshop wherein are fashioned all plans created by man . . . and man can create anything which he can imagine," writes Napoleon Hill, author of *Think and Grow Rich*. Learning to *train* your imagination to work for you on the goals you have decided to achieve can move you ahead to every success you have ever desired.

When I decided that I had to make some changes in life, I began to visualize the kind of life that would make me happy. I always saw myself engaged in work that was stimulating, required continued learning, and involved interesting people. Scrubbing floors and cleaning ovens just never came up on my mental screen. Somehow I had to pull myself out of the role of homemaker and into some kind of work outside the home. The four months of part-time work as a television co-host during my senior year in college offered all the elements I wanted in a job. I liked the people, the constant flow of new information; I liked the tension, that pang of "living on the edge." And I admit that I liked the attention. But how to stop looking like a "little mommy" and start looking and feeling like a television talent? I began by visualizing myself in the role of a television personality. Actually, visualization was the key factor in my goal-setting process, for I had to "try on" several options I'd been considering. It's much easier if you know what you want early in life, set down goals, and methodically work toward their attainment. But at thirty-six I was attempting a radical change and setting up a goal that was virtually impossible to achieve by all the standard means. However, I knew that I could manage the work if I could just land the job, and although twelve years had passed since my brief college experience with live television, I so passionately wanted that career that I was willing to learn whatever was necessary to "catch up." But to make it all happen would require a minor miracle. That is just what visualization can do.

I must admit that in the beginning I didn't recognize visualization as a technique; it was more like daydreaming. At the time, I was so discontented with my life the way it was that I would imagine myself working in a television studio or in an office near the studio. In my mind I would be wearing business clothes. Since I didn't own those kinds of clothes, I bought what I imagined myself wearing—a gray suit and gray shoes. I imagined myself sitting at a desk, answering the phone, walking into a studio. Later, when I was actually wearing my new business "look," it felt natural because I had been looking like that and behaving professionally in my mind for months.

I used visualization to change more than my "look." When I watched television I visualized myself on the screen, then in my mind I went behind the screen into the studio and saw myself looking into the lens of the camera. It took more effort and concentration, but I also managed to imagine myself, from inside myself, doing it. I tried to re-create in my mind what it would be like inside my skin, actually sitting there, smiling at the camera, reading, talking to the floor crew, waiting for the red light to come on. While preparing me for my quest for the job, that early visualization reinforced my goal and fueled my determination to achieve it.

It wasn't until I discovered *Psycho-Cybernetics* by Maxwell Maltz, M.D., that I realized the truly mind-boggling phenomenon I had picked up. Maltz explains why "mental picturing" produces such astonishing results. He writes, "Your nervous system cannot tell the difference between an actual experience and one that is vividly imagined." Maltz explains that the brain and the nervous system automatically work together as a "guidance system" to achieve the target goals it is programmed to reach. He compares the mechanism to a "self-aiming torpedo" as it seeks the goal you have told it to achieve. Your unconscious efforts will move you to people, information, activities, experiences that are on your goal trajectory. Once you clearly decide what you want, much of the work is automatically carried on by your "autopilot." By clearly seeing in your mind the picture of what you want to have, become, achieve, the automatic goal-finder mechanism kicks into gear. It must have a vivid image, the more detailed the better—colors, sounds, smells, feelings. And it must be reinforced regularly, with consistency.

◆ *Kid's Play Works!*

Dr. Maltz tells us that successful men and women have been using "mental pictures" since the beginning of time.

We marvel at a child's vivid imagination and his early ability to pretend with such detail. How many cases do you know of children who actually grew up to be what they spent years pretending or visualizing? Napoleon practiced "soldiering" in his imagination for years before he actually went into battle. As a youngster, Conrad Hilton pretended he was a hotel operator, and he continued to imagine himself running hotels before he bought one.

Television entertainer Ed McMahon, who is probably best

known as Johnny Carson's sidekick on NBC's *Tonight Show,* decided when he was a kid that he wanted to be in broadcasting. In a personal interview he told me that he began to envision himself as an announcer. "All my heroes were announcers. When I was alone, I would hold a flashlight as though it were a microphone, and read *Time* magazine to my little dog." Ed McMahon is one of the best-known announcers on the air today.

The story of Steve DeVore of Hayward, California, is one I've kept in my office file for several years. When Steve DeVore was two and a half years old he was stricken with polio and told he would never walk again. His parents must have had an insight into the powers of the visual mind. They told little Steve to imagine a war going on in his muscles. Every time he felt pain he was told to visualize the good antibodies waging war against the "bad germs," with the antibodies winning each battle. Within a year Steve amazed the doctors by regaining full use of his paralyzed muscles. He grew into a fine young athlete, and as a senior in high school he was offered baseball scholarships to three universities.

That experience stayed with him, for in the mid-seventies psychologist Steve DeVore initiated a research program called Sybervision, sponsored by the Professional Development Associates of Hayward, California. Steve took two members of the Cal State tennis team and videotaped their normal performance over a period of time. Next he edited the videotape to include only the best examples of their skills. He then taught the athletes relaxation techniques, making them receptive to visual and physical suggestion. On a life-sized television screen, in a quiet room, each athlete watched himself, in complete relaxation, perform the perfect serve, the perfect return, over and over. DeVore guided each player to "absorb" the images of himself performing flawlessly until a belief in that perfection became etched in the mind. The athletes were taught to cue their mental tape for playback during an actual match. In just two weeks both players made the starting five. Both finished the tennis season with perfect records and placed high in the national competition.

◆ Visualization Can Change Your Life!

DeVore's techniques were highly innovative for the mid-seventies. Now there are many companies that incorporate even more sophisticated techniques and technology. Computer animation can track every segment of a movement. In slow motion, line graphics and the video camera can isolate every subtlety of performance and technique. But as evidenced in hundreds of personal accounts, it is not necessary to hire a visualization coach, a psychologist, or a videotape company. Visualization can be learned from reading this chapter and from practicing these techniques.

I met Jessica Mitchell several years ago when I was producing a fashion segment for *The Today Show*. It had been a dreadful winter, and I wanted something really bright and hopeful for my early January Lifestyle segment. I found that the new swimwear was arriving at all the major department stores and decided that skimpy swimsuits on gorgeous models with tropical music would be the perfect way to warm up a morning that was expected to hit 3 below.

After a series of phone calls I found the perfect spokesperson: Jessica Mitchell, the associate fashion director of Saks Fifth Avenue. She knew everything about swimsuit fabric, design, accessories, and designer names, and she was very enthusiastic. I liked her from the moment I heard her voice on the phone. When we met at Saks to select swimsuits, she was seated the whole time, and it wasn't until we discussed the details of her studio appearance that she mentioned that she had to walk on crutches. Jessica explained that she had arthritis, and that it would continue to progress until she would probably no longer be able to work. It saddened me. She was so attractive and looked as if she were only in her early thirties. The crutches made no difference in her *Today* appearance since there would be no walking on or off the set while the cameras rolled. Several months later I was working on another fashion spot, and naturally I called Jessica, only to discover that she had taken a four-month leave of absence from Saks. I sadly interpreted that to mean that Jessica's condition had deteriorated, and I wondered about her chances of returning to a job so full of pressure and tension. When January rolled around the next year I decided to produce another swimwear segment similar to our very successful past effort. To my utter amazement Jessica Mitchell was back at Saks, and she'd been promoted! When I arrived at her office to work out the final selection of suits and models, I couldn't believe my eyes.

Jessica was walking around as if she had never had a problem. When we had a private moment I asked what miracle had taken place. She explained that she had gone to a clinic to learn relaxation, visualization, and biofeedback techniques. She said it had changed her life. She learned to use her mind to control her nervous tension, pain, and joint stiffness, and she continues to use the techniques as part of her ongoing therapy.

Several weeks later I had lunch with Jessica and she looked terrific. She was soon to be married, about to move into a new apartment, and her career was blooming. Jessica learned to tap and train her powers of visualization to correct her debilitating health problem and to enrich her life.

◆ Visualization Fitness

Visualization is a powerful way to help you realize your goals. I've found that those who consciously use it have different styles of application, but the objective is the same, and the results are astonishing. It may require some initial experimentation to discover the technique that is right for you.

In every instance applied visualization begins with relaxation. No impression is going to "stick" on the conscious or unconscious mind if you are "uptight," too tired, distracted by problems or irritations, or physically uncomfortable. You cannot focus and concentrate if there are loud noises or interruptions—like the phone ringing or the stove timer going off. It takes a few sessions before you get the system down, but it's worth the investment.

After the birth of my second son, I had to get serious about my exercise program. The body doesn't just "pop" back into shape. Each morning I had to push the furniture back to make room. I had to change into the right clothes. I had to get a stack of books for my sidebends. I had to open my exercise book to the photograph demonstrating the exercises for my "problem area." It was a big production. After a while, though, it became routine. I no longer needed to consult the book, I discovered exercise positions that required less furniture shuffling, and I scheduled my sessions in the morning before I got dressed, eliminating the hassle of changing clothes. I took the telephone off the hook and in very little time my exercise session became as routine as making the morning coffee.

◆ Your Success Fitness Plan

Your visualization exercises work the same way. Think of them as a fitness plan for success. You may not see the pounds drop off (although some have used visualization to enhance their weight-loss program, imagining themselves as slender, wearing a size 8, passing up desserts and bread), but you will see and feel yourself moving toward your goals and getting there!

The following is my basic visualization technique, but there are as many variations as people. Find what works best for you.

1. Set aside thirty minutes each day for quiet concentration. As you become more adept, you may require only twenty minutes. See that you will not be interrupted or distracted.

2. Lie down or position yourself in a comfortable lounger, allowing your head to lean back on a pillow or support with your legs extended. Loosen any tight clothing. Close your eyes.

3. Begin to relax by taking a really slow, deep breath. Hold it for a count of five, exhale slowly. Do this at least three times. On days when you are particularly tense you may require five deep breaths. While you are breathing clear your mind of the details and concerns of the day by thinking of your favorite "secret" place, like a deserted, sunlit beach, a glorious meadow filled with wildflowers, a sparkling mountain brook, whatever you perceive to be the most peaceful sanctuary. As you relax more completely, exercise your imagination and fill out the picture—add smells and sounds. Feel the warm

sand under your feet, smell the fragrant air, feel the wind on your face, the sun warming your body.

4. Let go of your body. Relax your jaw. Chances are that it is rigid and set. Let your shoulders droop, your fingers unfold, and go limp. Let your legs become so relaxed that you are unaware of them. Release your facial muscles and let your face become smooth and young and carefree. Listen to your natural breathing. Let your sense of time and place slip away.

5. Now think about your goal in vivid, living color. See yourself achieving your goal, assuming the new responsibility and rewards, accepting accolades. In your mind you are living your goal. What are you wearing? What car are you driving? What is your office like? How do you act? It is essential that you fully assume the behavior of your new role. Fill in the details, create a scene. Do not allow your mind to click back. At first it's bound to happen. You may suddenly find yourself thinking about what to have for dinner or when to wash the car. Immediately return to your special scene. I find that one way to avoid these intrusions is to continue to add details to the picture.

When you have completed your success scene, and you are feeling fulfilled and victorious and satisfied, close the scenario and slowly drift back to the reality of the day. You really will feel more relaxed and confident, as renewed as you feel when you come out of a wonderful movie. Remember, your mental movie moves you toward your goals.

◆ Simulation

The imagination has no limits. We can imagine ourselves owning a one-hundred-foot yacht, or laden with Cartier jewelry, but there are laws against actually rehearsing those scenes. However, there will be situations that call for taking the mental rehearsal on to physical rehearsal, actually going through the motions physically. The astronauts use simulation for months, sometimes years, before an actual space mission. Student drivers practice in a mock automobile. Business schools conduct simulated interviews to prepare students for actual job interviews. Simulating an event or situation is always the best preparation and is another technique used by high achievers.

Throughout my career many people, including my producers, have remarked that I was a "natural." Believe me, there is nothing less natural than sitting in a huge, dark, cold television studio with blinding lights in your eyes, talking to something that resembles an X-ray machine while microphone cables are taped under your blouse. And it can't be just talking, but "chatting," as if you're talking to your best friend or neighbor all the while a dark figure hunkers near a camera giving you strange time signals. While you're talking "naturally," you have to figure out how you are going to stop (or get your guest to stop) talking when your time runs out, and do it *naturally!*

The WCPO-TV audition in Cincinnati was the opportunity of a lifetime, and I was terrified. I visualized and persisted my way into the chance, but could I pull it off? As I awkwardly rehearsed the newscast and feature report, I realized that I needed to gain more confidence, needed to feel more natural. So I instinctively carried visualization to the next step: simulation. Obviously, I couldn't afford to rent a television studio for my rehearsals, but I tried to construct the setting with what I had on hand. I set up my 35-mm camera with a chair in front and practiced reading to the smaller camera. I changed the position of the camera during the day and practiced talking to it, treating it like a person, becoming comfortable in its presence. The boys thought I had blown my switch when they saw me stop and converse with our family camera, but now I know that may have made the difference in my real on-camera performance. I got the job, and my life began to move swiftly toward what I wanted.

Nearly two years later I landed another audition, this time with WABC-TV, the ABC-owned television station in New York. I was to write and anchor a newscast. I was to deliver their copy the day before to be transferred to the teleprompter. I had never before used a teleprompter! Furthermore, I was absolutely baffled at how anyone could even see the words that far away and not only read it as if they were "just talking," but read it while it was moving! And what if the teleprompter operator stopped moving my copy? I was doomed. It would have been easier if it were something I liked and wanted to learn, but I had a dread of the prompter. It could make a fool of me—expose me. Again, I resorted to what I knew worked.

Roger, my close friend and chief support (now my husband), went to the butcher shop and bought a long roll of butcher paper. With a Magic Marker I transferred the entire ABC newscast to the paper. Then we opened the door of an old dish cabinet I'd refinished during my "hobbies" career. Roger slowly pulled the copy over the door as I sat some distance away reading and timing with a stopwatch.

At first I squinted and stumbled. When I became more familiar with the copy, I sounded as if I were reading the newspaper to a room full of elderly people. Then I had to learn to pretend I was reading from the papers I held in my hand by looking down and back up, catching the copy on the rolling paper at just the right spot! More than once I muttered, "There's got to be a better way to earn a living."

I can't tell you how many times I went over that moving roll of butcher paper. It seemed like hundreds—poor Roger's arm was about to drop off. But when I arrived at ABC Studios for my audition I felt prepared, and I also had the self-confidence to ask for a run-through. I wanted to be comfortable in the chair, get the feeling of the real teleprompter, and give the prompter operator an opportunity to hear my reading speed and style of pauses. It went off without a hitch, and later, as I watched the playback, I was once again flabbergasted that it was actually me looking like the real thing!

◆◆

Visualization is your powerful goal "guidance system."
- Train your imagination to use visualization techniques.
- Each day practice your visualization exercises and your fitness program according to the steps outlined in this chapter.
- See yourself actually going through the emotions of achieving your goal.
- See yourself in your mind living as though you had already achieved your goal.

Whenever possible, reinforce visualization with simulation.
- Use simulation as a rehearsal technique—as preparation for new experiences.
- Set up a mock situation with props and equipment suggesting the real thing.

◆◆

Visualization is truly the ultimate mind-altering and behavior-altering experience. You can get what you want; you can make it to your goals. It all begins with visualization.

5

◆

Take Risks

---

*If you create a life
that is always comfortable, always
without risk, you have only created
a fool's paradise.*

—DAVID VISCOTT, M.D.

IT WAS A stinging cold February. Cincinnati was experiencing the worst winter in decades. The moving van had barely made it down the narrow, drifted lane to pick up the household goods that had been tagged as mine. Bill and I had made a complete inventory of everything in the house and had calmly initialed each item so that both would get what was "fair." I gave up the waffle iron for the blender, the color television for the stereo, the beds in the guest room for the queen-size in our room.

We were embarking on a "great adventure," I told my nine-year-old son Billy bravely as we drove to the Ramada Inn on I-75. I'm quite sure he didn't buy that. The roads were covered with ice, and a fine, icy mist blew across the highway. The whole winter world seemed dark and threatening. The next morning we were to begin our long drive to Princeton, New Jersey, where we would move into a small apartment and settle down to the "transition." I was quaking inside; I was taking the biggest risk of my life.

To my utter dismay and panic, WCPO-TV canceled *In Person* two weeks *after* my divorce was final. Unfortunately, the monthly alimony/child support amount I received had been determined by using my WCPO salary as a base income. At the time I was proud that I would not be a financial burden to Bill. I'd received several thousand dollars from the sale of my half interest in the house, but I considered that "security" money, not living money. Since the monthly alimony/child support payments alone would not be enough to live on, I knew that my "security" would run out pretty quickly without a regular salary. The thought of going back to Bill and the court only two weeks later to plead for more money was repugnant to me, so I began looking for alternatives, utterly terrified.

In Person had actually been quite successful. It was even nominated for a national programming award, and the local television critics praised my contribution. One even called me a "diamond in the rough." The program had simply not made any money. When the station's general manager called me into his office to break the news to me privately, he said, "Nancy, I have some good news and some bad news. *In Person* is being canceled, but Nancy Foreman is *not* being canceled." How thoroughly considerate of him!

I would be assigned to the news department and assume the duties of a regular street reporter. Interpretation: "It would be bad press to fire you, so we'll throw you down to the news grinder . . . and you won't last long there, baby!" Just as I suspected, "down there" became an exercise in survival rather than the sound news experience that I needed. Finally it became clear that if indeed I was to survive, I had to move on. There was too much history, I'd spent too much time in Cincinnati as Mrs. Connell to be perceived as a professional. I had to have a fresh start. So there I was with an adorable nine-year-old in his navy-blue hooded storm suit, an apricot toy poodle, and as many plants as I could fit in the car, starting out on the next chapter of my life with storm warnings on the car radio every fifteen minutes. One look at the sky and I knew that we were headed into heavy snow. For me, the storms of risk lasted five months.

My older son, Jeff, then thirteen, chose to stay with Bill in Cincinnati, and although I was crushed that we would be separated, I knew that what I had to do would be tough enough with a nine-year-old and a dog. A resentful thirteen-year-old in the throes of adolescence could reduce my chances from slim to impossible. I resolved to get Jeff to join us after our life settled into some kind of routine. In the meantime, we would stay in close contact through frequent calls and letters and as many visits as we could arrange.

My lifeline was Roger, who had guided me through the WCPO-TV ordeal, brought me *Broadcasting* magazine, and showed me how to study the "help wanted" classified ads. He helped me update my resume and pull together a folder of *In Person* press coverage and photographs, and instructed me to locate a videotape editor to make a composite tape of my *In Person* segments. He bought me books on the industry, brought me newspaper clippings from other markets, and continually affirmed me as a person. Although I had grave doubts about my future in television, he would not let me waver but fiercely insisted that I *did* have talent and that the cancelation of *In Person* was an economic decision and not a reflection on my skills and abilities.

I was in no shape emotionally to see that my "lifeline" had a few weaknesses, and that my Princeton adventure could easily turn into a nightmare in which two drowning souls tried to save each other. Roger was taking a big risk, too. He had left his prestigious position with the University of Cincinnati and set forth to chop his way into the competitive world of private business as a television consultant and producer. He was still recovering from his divorce, had custody of his adopted seven-year-old daughter, Jennifer, had considerable post-divorce debts, and was, in fact, clinging to me as fiercely as I was to him.

The plan was that in Princeton I would assist Roger in setting up his consulting practice for a salary while I looked for a job in New York. That way I would have a base of operations and Billy would attend a fine school. I would also have the flexibility to commute to New York, an hour-long train ride from Princeton, whenever I landed an audition or interview. Roger was eager for us to marry, or even live together, but I would rather have driven in a demolition derby than join a man who was healing and groping for a "place" just as desperately as I was. So we got together for dinner several times a week. We took the children on weekend day trips to the ocean, did laundry, and swapped baby-sitters. I helped at his office to establish a filing system, research television awards for a client, and handle his messages when I wasn't making the rounds of agents and television contacts.

It was the darkest time in my life. I had to borrow from my "security" each month to make ends meet. The cost of living in Princeton left me reeling, and the price of commuter train tickets, car insurance, and taxicabs were all new expenses for me. Billy was a real trouper. I signed up for the Big Brother Program at Princeton University so Billy would have a college student to spend time with on Saturdays or Sundays. That gave me a break and Billy a role model and substitute brother. My eyes filled with tears the first time the student called saying, "I'm with the Big Brother . . ." I had always associated that kind of thing with orphans or poor people, and not *my* son. Another time, when I took Billy to his soccer practice in Princeton, I was handed a routine information form to complete. I got to the line requesting the telephone number of a neighbor, friend, or family member who should be contacted if I couldn't be reached in case of an emergency. My armor crumbled and I burst into tears. There was *no one* I could list. I didn't know my neighbors, there was no family within hundreds of miles, and Roger was traveling or in New York much of the time.

Each time the train returned me to Princeton after a day of brutal New York–style rejection, I would be in a total panic worrying about Billy. Could he have lost his key? Let in some stranger? Left the stove on? What if he had been hit by a baseball at school? I had been out of contact all day, and by the time I reached the apartment I would be wild with worry. He was always smiling, watching television, baking cookies, or building a model plane. I'd collapse in a chair and thank the Lord that we'd made it through another day.

It soon became clear that Roger could no longer afford to

pay me my original salary; I really wasn't earning it, anyway. I did land a couple of auditions, but in each case there would be no decision for several weeks. *Nothing* was happening fast enough . . . this arrangement wasn't working. And my courage was failing me. I was now the head of our little family, so I took charge and made a decision. I announced to Roger that two sinking ships did not equal one afloat, and that I would begin to look for work outside the area. It meant that we would be separated, but so be it. My first responsibility was to my son and myself. If we were to have a life together, it could only happen after we had each found independence and established our own identities. I needed his help and support to begin the search, but I would manage without him if need be. That was a real turning point.

Roger arranged an appointment with the news director for the CBS-owned television stations. I explained up front that I only wanted his advice, not a job (although that would have been nice). He was blunt about my chances of finding a television job in New York in view of my weak employment record. "You'll have to prove yourself in the field," he said. "New York would gobble you up. Talk to an agent who specializes in out-of-town talent placement."

Before I left his office he phoned the top out-of-town agent and set up an appointment for me. That's when things began to happen *fast*. My composite tape was sent to WKBW-TV in (of all places) Buffalo, New York. I was flown up for an audition, accepted their offer, and faced another big risk.

There would be hardships. It would mean another move for Billy, leaving Roger, my sole support system, setting up life in a totally unfamiliar place (I did not know a single person in Buffalo). But my real anxiety was that it had been twelve years since my brief encounter with live television. My more recent television experience had been on videotape. *A.M. Buffalo,* the show I was to co-host, was a live one-hour talk show with emphasis on in-studio guests and viewer telephone questions. Actually, Buffalo posed a bigger risk. I could fail miserably, be rejected by the viewers and local critics, be dumped by the station at the end of my one-year contract, and have nowhere to go but *down.* And there was no way to test the market quietly. Every word, expression, attitude, and mistake was right out there for the whole world to see and judge. I would be aware of that every time I opened my mouth.

Later I will share some of the terrors of that first month on *A.M. Buffalo,* but now it's important to know that the risk, and it was a big one, *turned my life around.* The two-year Buffalo experience was probably the richest of my life. I not only proved myself in the television profession, I proved my independence by managing my own home (I bought a condominium by myself!). I was solely responsible for raising my son and managing my career, which was demanding. It was a wonderful time, and I ultimately moved from Buffalo, the twenty-eighth television market, to the network, which had never before been accomplished by a Buffalo talent. The standard course is to move from one market to another, from Buffalo to Chicago or Los Angeles, before ever being considered ready for New York.

I can't imagine what direction my life would have taken had I not pursued and accepted the risks of moving to Princeton and the unknown, then on to Buffalo and the known but terrifyingly real world of daily broadcasts. Living and working on my own helped me carve out a new identity for myself and for others. Until I became an experienced television co-host, I didn't trust my own abilities, for there had been little chance to test them, measure them in the marketplace. This was do or die—live on the salary, manage all the responsibilities for myself and Billy. I found that there really are no shortcuts. The only way to find out what you can do is to do it: take the risk!

◆ Risks: The Big Choices

I define risks as the big choices in life: the major decisions involving job changes, where to live, whom to marry, whether to invest in a new business. We deal with decisions and challenges regularly, but a risk occurs when the stakes are high and the outcome will be noticed. These are the events that can move us ahead by leaps and bounds. These are the events that count!

We all know people who are committed to maintaining the status quo, the ones who make every effort to *avoid risks.*

In doing so they limit their growth; they cannot live to the fullest. But the real tragedy is that they can never discover their true capabilities, their personal peaks and valleys.

A good friend who has been with NBC a number of years as a behind-the-camera producer has been trying desperately to move into on-camera work. She had prepared a couple of auditions for *The Today Show* which proved to be very good. However, on every occasion she was told that although she had potential she would have to build her new identity in another area. (Interpretation: Go to Buffalo!) Network producers are not going to take a chance on someone who pulls together a one-shot audition. When I explained how to contact an agent who specializes in nationwide placement, my friend paled and cried, "Move from New York! I could end up in Davenport, Iowa, or Kansas City! And do you know what they pay out there? How can you live on twenty or thirty thousand dollars a year?"

I went through all the reasons why a couple of years in another city was the best way (and, in this case, the only way) for her to achieve her goal. I explained how the cost of living was much lower "out there," that $20,000 goes a long way, and how I did it very comfortably. The quality of life is better, the people are friendlier, and everything is closer and easier to negotiate. She couldn't accept the risk. Or perhaps she had a weak commitment to her goal. What I witnessed was that moment of decision that makes the difference between a high achiever and one who will continue at the same level, probably becoming more discontent and moaning bitterly that life is unfair.

"Not risking is the surest way of losing," writes psychiatrist David Viscott in his book, *Risking*. He explains that many people have a kind of risk "paralysis" and seek relationships, jobs, organizations that offer security and stability. Viscott is clear about the necessity of taking risks. He says if a risk is "comfortable," it is not worth taking, and that you have probably outgrown it. There really is no substitute for taking risks. You can do all the homework, get advice from others, study ways others take risks, but you have to take the risk yourself or there is nothing to be gained. You have to stick your neck out, put yourself on the line, go for broke. I had to go to Buffalo!

Risks are uncomfortable because we're afraid. When I pulled up stakes and moved to Princeton, I was afraid that I wouldn't find a job, that my money would run out, that I would be lonely, that I would be rejected in the market which would devastate my newborn professional "posture." My fears were compounded because my nine-year-old son was included in my risk taking. Would he make new friends, do well in school? How badly would he miss his brother and father? Would he stay healthy? I had come a long way from deciding which floor covering would be best for the kitchen. This was the big risk. Psychologists may call them "uncomfortable," but let me tell you I was feeling raw terror! At the time I would not have been able to list all those fears as I did just now. Instead, I became tense, I didn't sleep well, I probably overindulged Billy. Now I better understand taking risks and the value of knowing the related fears.

◆ Risks: The Big Fears

1. FEAR OF LOSS: Risks can bring possible loss—of money, property, control, position, or title, and the accompanying loss of respect. What else can I say? This is heavy loss.

2. FEAR OF THE UNKNOWN: Not everyone has the spirit of the explorer. Setting off for a new world, sampling new experiences, gathering new information, once again being a newcomer, means facing new frontiers with only our own resources to pull us through.

3. FEAR OF EXPOSURE: Risks mean vulnerability. Risks will expose our real intelligence, skills, talents, strength, character, whatever the case may be. And that's terrifying. We could be embarrassed, humiliated, we could lose self-esteem. And that could set us back in our pursuit.

4. FEAR OF BEING HURT: The fear of being hurt is so great that many people cannot allow themselves to be completely open and vulnerable in a love relationship.

5. FEAR OF REJECTION: Our need to be accepted, loved, and admired is very strong, and many avoid taking risks

because of the possible emotional upheaval. For several years I avoided asking the cleaning woman to clean under the refrigerator because I was afraid she wouldn't like me. Then I figured out that life isn't a popularity contest, and while it is better to get along with people, it's also necessary to risk rejection to get the job done or to get on to the next phase.

6. FEAR OF CHANGE: Whenever we take risks, we are somehow changed by the experience. We leave the familiar and move ahead. It's a kind of departure—from job, community, home security, the known. Risks force us to cut new paths, and one of the fears is that we are not only leaving familiar people and places, we are leaving a phase of ourselves behind. We will be different, know more, be more experienced, tougher, wiser, in some way changed by the encounter.

When I think of the raw essence of risk, I remember my Jeff, when he was three, shivering, little swim trunks drooping, crouched at the edge of the pool, trying to get up the nerve to jump into my arms. It wouldn't count if someone pushed him or if I reached up and lifted him in. He had to jump on his own, make the decision, take the chance, feel the moment of being out of control, trust that I would catch him, and accept the praise, the sense of satisfaction and confidence that come with a successful leap.

◆ Rules of Risk-Taking

Taking adult risks works the same way. There are steps to taking risks. Learn the process, become familiar with the right way to approach and evaluate risks. Learn the smart risk taker's rules.

1. ASSESS: Evaluate the risk. What do you have to gain? What do you have to lose? Consider the worst thing that could happen and decide if you could live with it. Write down everything you have to gain and everything you could lose.

Size up the situation, check the odds, find out who and what is involved. Prepare for the "known" part, and the unknown will be less intimidating. Viscott cautions us, however, that "no risk worth taking can ever be made completely secure, no matter what technology is at your disposal. The unknown can never be made certain." That's what makes it a risk.

2. ACT: Take the plunge. After you have weighed the pros and cons and decided to take the risk, move on it. Many risks fail because too much time is spent in procrastination. As Viscott warns, "Don't sit back and wait for the perfect moment. It almost never comes."

3. TRUST: Let go. Accept the fact that you will be out of control for a time. It is the time between the jump and being caught. It is the helplessness of the pitcher after he releases the ball. Nothing can be done while the ball travels to the batter. This is the time between takeoff and landing, and for many it is the most harrowing. After you have applied for the transfer, completed the forms, been interviewed, you wait.

4. CLOSURE: This is it. The race is over, the reviews are in, you're adjusting to the new community, job, or acquisition. This is the time to accept the praise and accolades. This is what risk is all about. This is the "high" that draws people to risk. We get measured or tested; we know more about ourselves, and whatever the outcome, we have grown. We find out how good we are or what we need to work on.

Win, lose, or draw, just taking the risk and seeing it through is an accomplishment of which to be proud. You did it!

Although risks mean big change and high stakes, it's good to maintain perspective and not panic or develop acid indigestion. As Ed McMahon put it, a bit of a "devil-may-care" attitude helps.

He tells the story about the time he applied for a job as a surveyor with the War Department. He had always been fascinated by surveyors, and since he had some time before he had to report for duty, he figured he could learn the business from the bottom.

"When I went in to see the interviewer, I was asked if I'd ever been a rodman. I was just a kid, and I didn't know what the hell a rodman was, but I figured it was best to follow my father's advice—'Act like you know what you're doing'—so I said, 'Yes!'

"In the middle of the interview a crew chief came storming into the office, all upset because he had to get a rodman to fill out his crew.

" 'I'm hiring one right now,' the interviewer replied.

" 'Hire him later and let him come with me now!' the chief said.

"Before you knew it I was in the chief's pickup and on my way to the job site. I realized that I had better level with the chief.

" 'Sir,' I said, 'there's something I have to tell you before we get started. I really don't know much about being a rodman. But if you'll give me one day, I'll be the best rodman you ever had.' "

This is where Ed hardens his face and tells how the chief glowered at him with murder in his eye, then spit and adjusted his hat. Since he was shorthanded he agreed to give Ed a chance. You can probably fill in the rest. Ed not only kept his job as a rodman, but when the chief got sick six weeks later, guess who took over the crew? As Ed said, he took the risk, got in on a bluff, but was able to pull it off anyway. Nothing ventured, nothing gained.

Aviatrix and superbusinesswoman Brooke Knapp is another model risk taker. She makes a list of her fears every year. Then she makes one of her goals to conquer those fears. For a long time she was terrified of flying, but she was determined to overcome it. She took lessons and not only conquered the fear but became an expert pilot, setting twenty aviation speed records. An innocent dinner conversation inspired her to take a big risk. Her friends were complaining about the poor air service to California cities, and Brooke saw the business potential. Before the evening was over she had agreed to buy a plane for inner-California passenger service if her friends agreed to contract for a given number of hours. She pulled together a tax-shelter group to finance her eight-seat jet. That was four years ago. Today Brooke Knapp is president and chairman of Jet Airways, a five-million-dollar charter air service. She employs nineteen pilots, contracts about six hundred hours a month, and spends at least forty hours a month in the cockpit herself. "If I didn't take some sort of risk, life would lose interest," she notes.

Don't be afraid to take your *own* risks; then you can write your own story. Nothing will bring you as much satisfaction and pride. Learn to take risks. They can be the most exciting events of your life, as you soar toward your goals.

6

♦

Polish Your Steel

Without persistence, you will be defeated,
even before you start.
With persistence you will win.

—NAPOLEON HILL, *Think and Grow Rich*

SHORTLY AFTER ROGER and I decided to get married, he introduced me to his longtime friend, a man whose experience and wisdom he admired. I immediately responded to his friend's intelligence, wit, and warmth. Much later Roger told me that John had given him a friendly warning: "Watch out, Roger; there's steel in that lady." That opened a discussion on personal "steel" that has continued for five years. I've questioned others that have it; I've asked psychologists to define it. I've observed the resignation of those who lack it, and I remember the times that "steel" was being painfully forged in myself.

It was late July 1978 when I rolled into Buffalo's Holiday Inn with a carload of plants, clothes, the dog, and whatever I'd forgotten to pack for the movers. I had no place to live, and the three or four people I had met in Buffalo were my new employers, not friends I could go to screaming for help. I was the new co-host for their most important live production. I was a professional; I was independent. And oh, was I *scared*. Billy had been safely sent to the same summer camp he had attended the previous year, which was a tremendous relief, for I had to focus all my energies toward developing a new skill. My entire career depended on it.

The male co-host had come to Buffalo from a news anchor position in Los Angeles, and although a live television veteran, he had never before hosted a magazine program. For a week the two of us would observe the *A.M. Buffalo* program (using substitutes from the news department), then spend the afternoon lining up guests for the following week, when we would take over.

The station had agreed to pay for my meals and lodging for ten days. After that, I was on my own. It made sense to buy a condominium, something more permanent. It was time to put down some roots and establish a home for Billy and me, a place where Jeff would feel secure and comfortable visiting. Roger came to Buffalo for a weekend of house hunting. He helped me find just the right condo, but it wouldn't be available for a whole month! Roger hurried back to Princeton and his business, and I began the depressing search for an interim place to rent. The nicer apartments were full, and they wouldn't accept animals—even a toy poodle. With lower lip quivering, I checked into my last resort, the Abington Manor. It was just what I had always imagined a flophouse would look and smell like—dusty, musty, a sagging bed with wood veneer headboard and a faded blue chenille spread. There was a dank little kitchenette in the corner and a bath with dripping plumbing and thin (often torn) towels. Thank heaven Billy and Jeff or my friends back in Cincinnati didn't see me like this.

When I sat on the bed, struggling to hold back my tears, a leg snapped off. I replaced it with two phone directories. I set up April's doggie dish and bed in the corner, arranged my plants around the one window, and tried to cheer myself. At least this would cut down on the wild sex orgies I supposed my married friends had envisioned for this divorced, slightly aging sex kitten. Nevertheless, it was hardly the appropriate setting for a television personality! Besides, what I had to do had nothing whatsoever to do with my living conditions.

If Princeton was the darkest time of my life, that first month in Buffalo was the most strenuous. I have never worked harder, struggled more desperately, or been more exhausted. I was astounded that my co-host could be so glib. He could ad-lib, relate experiences, pick up on almost any remark, and turn it all into talk! I later found out that he had once been a disc jockey. Still, I found myself staring at his mouth, amazed at his deep resonant voice and the ease with which whole coherent paragraphs seemed to effortlessly tumble forth. Then he would turn to me and say, "What about you, Nancy . . . did you ever make ice cream from scratch?" I would be tongue-tied, my mouth would suddenly dry up, and the first sound out of me was usually, "Uh . . ." I was embarrassed that my speech was slower and halting; I sounded stupid! I had opinions and interesting experiences, but they weren't pulling together into nice, neat little one- and two-minute packages. I was certain that people must be calling me "Buffalo's Barbie Doll."

The only thing to do was to push up my sleeves and dig in. When I returned to my little hovel, I would begin my preparation for the next day. I practiced the names of the guests over and over. "Helen Grabowski (Grab-ou-skee) joins us now for some great ideas on updating those old wide-lapeled blazers." Each day we interviewed four guests, and each evening I read everything I could find on them; I wrote introductions and at least a dozen questions for each. I wrote lines of transition leading to taped segments or jackpot phone calls. I wrote everything I thought I would have to say.

Each night there was something new to practice and something new to fear. Buffalo is a city full of Indian, Italian, German, and Polish names, the likes of which I had never heard in Nebraska! Over and over I would say, "Scajaquada Parkway," "Martin Wasaluski," then I would use them in context, trying to make them roll off my tongue. What most people, including me, don't realize is that all that "talk" has to be carefully organized in your head. It doesn't just pour out. I wrote out everything in longhand and rehearsed it until it sounded conversational, leaving room for spontaneous reactions to Brian, my co-host, or to a guest or caller. Then I would try to anticipate their responses, so that I could have something to say. There was no teleprompter. We had to "wing it."

It took six months before my mouth worked as fast as Brian's, before I trusted that my experiences and opinions would be as interesting as his, before I could reveal my humor and personality, which up until then I had kept carefully hidden, afraid that our viewers wouldn't like me or would find me dull.

But it was the internal "steel" that provided the reinforcement and the determination to make it work. I've come to define that kind of strength as the P.R.W. factor: *persistence, resilience,* and *work.* That magic trio directed toward achieving a goal cannot miss!

Fortunately I knew where to find my "steel" one morning about two years later when I was new on *The Today Show.* At that time the taped commercials were recorded *before* the program went on the air, which meant that I got up at 3:30 A.M., the limousine was to pick me up at 4:00 A.M., I would report for hair and makeup at 4:45 A.M., and tape would roll at 5:30 A.M. sharp! It was the first time that 20/20 Eyedrops had ever bought a commercial pool with our production department, so everyone was appropriately tense. I had rehearsed my part and felt comfortable with the script, but I began to get very nervous at 4:08 A.M. when the limo still hadn't arrived. Finally I called the dispatcher and was told that someone had called him earlier (what is earlier than 4:00 A.M.?) and canceled my car! There were five senior executives from the 20/20 Eyedrops firm who had flown in from Texas to watch the taping, and there were ad agency account people, plus our own NBC sales executives who were still sizing me up. And someone was playing games with my transportation into the city! I'd never before driven myself into Manhattan from our home in Dobbs Ferry, about nineteen miles north. What was I going to do . . . whine about the car not showing up or cry about someone being mean to me? I polished the "steel," got out our Westchester and Manhattan maps, and had Roger talk me through the driving directions, which I scribbled on the grocery pad. I set out in the pitch-black morning to prove that I was tough enough for the network, if I could just get there. I did. And I managed to stroll into the studio on time, coiffed and made-up for the taping.

PERSISTENCE, RESILIENCE, and WORK: These are the critical qualities that support the talent, creativity, vision, and leadership that we admire in others. Without the P.R.W. factor, those stellar qualities make little difference. I've heard other words used to describe essentially the same thing: fortitude, determination, grit, willpower, endurance, sticktoitiveness, discipline. Whatever the lexicon, it's the P.R.W. factor that turns *potential into product.*

◆ *Persistence*

Persistence is what makes the high achiever refuse to take "No" for an answer, to keep coming back, to keep looking for a "window." Like Maria declared in *The Sound of Music,* "When God closes all the doors, He always leaves a window open." It just takes persistence to *find* the window.

Persistence is what gets you through the "in betweens." Those are the tough times for many high achievers, for there is a momentum that comes with gearing up for the challenge, for making the big push. But we all know that every day can't be a red-letter day. There are miles of flat highways between the mountain ranges and rivers. Sometimes it seems like a long time between raises and promotions. The exhilaration of a live network camera doesn't last long, but there are long, lonely hours of preparation, tedious days in an editing room, boring afternoons on the telephone planning props, logistics, transportation.

Unless you can sustain the effort with consistency over the long haul, you will soon join the mass of short-termers. Dr. Charles Garfield, founder of the Performance Sciences Institute, has conducted extensive research on high achievers, and his studies indicate that "the ability to stick to it longer than anyone else is more important to success than innate ability or raw talent."

In this era of instant replays and computer printouts, we

have come to expect instant success. Woody Allen put it another way: "Ninety percent of life is just showing up!" Most people give up too easily or quit before they have given themselves a fair chance.

◆ *Resilience*

Resilience is the quality some call "thick-skinned," having a tough exterior. You've heard the expression "There's one tough cookie," or "She looks like she eats nails for breakfast." Being impervious to criticism and negative comments has nothing to do with the epidermis. Resilience doesn't have to show. Think of it as part of the inner steel that holds you together through all the storms, struggles, and setbacks you encounter along the road to success. It's the ability to make a mistake and "bounce back." It's knowing the difference between constructive and destructive criticism and being able to handle *both* without shattering. It's hearing all the reasons why something you want *cannot* be done, then deciding for yourself and going on to prove that it *can!* It's being unfazed by setbacks. It's being able to make a mistake, admit it, and go on without agonizing over it or being defeated. It's holding up under the strain.

Resilience is another trait that is learned over time. No one is born with resilience. It comes from taking risks, from some hard knocks, from being out there in the field of life. There is no way to learn resilience from the grandstands of life; you have to get out there on the field and get dirty! That's the only way to know how to pick yourself up, brush yourself off, and get back in the game.

The television business is perilous for the thin-skinned. I learned very quickly that if I was going to make it, I had better fortify my inner steel. I spent those early weeks co-hosting *A.M. Buffalo* constantly picking myself up! My most important undergarment became the heavy-duty dress shields. Every day I came off the air at 11:00 A.M. soaking wet with perspiration. Since the show had a trade agreement with a local department store, my on-air wardrobe was loaned for one appearance only in return for an on-air credit. Thank heaven for dress shields! After the show I would drink

chamomile tea to calm down and wait for the inevitable telephone calls criticizing my hair that day, objecting to something I'd asked a guest, or demanding that we "bring back
Jimmy's Polka Band." There wasn't time enough to dwell on
the caller's remarks, and I was too tired to cry.

When I got home, I had to be supportive to Billy and
his own transitions, and throw myself into preparations for
the next day. I fell asleep knowing that at 10:00 A.M. the next
morning the little red light would come on and I'd better be
ready. I was so tense and nervous that one of the station's
producers pulled me aside one day and said, "Nancy, you
would be a lot better if you could just relax. Why don't you
have a Bloody Mary before you go on, or a shot of something?
Or get your doctor to give you tranquilizers." My "red flare"
went up, and I determined then and there that if I ever needed
anything to get me up or calm me down, I had no business in
this line of work. And so far, I've done just fine without that
kind of "help." There isn't a television station in the country
that isn't haunted with tragic stories of talented people who
became sadly dependent on alcohol or drugs because they
lacked the resilience to cope with the pressure, vulnerability,
and the unexpected. Anyone who appears before the public
invites criticism, opposition, or just plain cheap shots. Once I
understood what I was feeling and why, I knew what to do:
polish my inner steel and draw on my resilience to make it
work!

I "toughened" up and quit worrying about criticism and
the threat of criticism or the possibility of making a complete
fool of myself. I made a private announcement: "This is who
I am, world. I'll do my best, but if you don't like it, I'm sorry.
I can't make myself crazy worrying about what you think of
me. I hope you're gentle, but if you're not, I can take it."

I settled down, my work improved, and the comments
from the outside became kinder. Although it was a welcome
turn of events, it really didn't matter that much, for I had
developed my own standard, set up my own expectations, and
that's what counts. The rest just rolled off like rain, which
reminds me of a comment made by the internationally known
batik artist Sara Eyestone, a woman whom I greatly admire.

When I asked Sara how she deals with negative comments and criticism about her work, she said, "I know what I want to create, and I do the best I can. If they don't like it, I feel that it's *their* problem. I like what I've done or I wouldn't show it. They have a right to their opinion, but I have the right to ignore them."

Sara is a woman of great resilience, and her struggle to become well known in her field is full of stories illustrating her inner steel. At one point she had to keep her budding career alive during a cross-country move. While she and her husband were waiting to close on their home, Sara lived in a Holiday Inn with her three children, two cats, and her cousin's two children. For an entire summer she cooked on a hot plate, washed dishes in the shower, and hauled clothes to a Laundromat while her husband went off to his new career. But Sara was determined not to let hardships keep her from her commitment to a one-woman show, which required a gallery full of her batik pieces.

Sara recalls, "We had a one-room motel room with the five kids. I had until September to pull together a one-woman show. I went out and bought supplies, and sat in this stuffy little mildewy room, painting like crazy. I had my beautiful batiks drying on the bushes of the motel. The whole show I was working on was hanging all around the motel and on the roof. It was hideous." The show opened on schedule to enthusiastic reviews, but probably no one sipping champagne and marveling at Sara's brilliant use of color and movement was aware of the hardships Sara overcame or the resilience of the woman who made it all look so easy.

Resilience is also the ability to deal with the unexpected without losing your balance. Sara's cross-country move didn't deter her from her commitment.

Then there was the time the roller derby came to town, and we decided to promote it by skating onto the set for the opening of the show. I hadn't been on skates since junior high school, but like a good sport I wobbled around on skates in a corner of the studio until it was time for the big entrance. Then, with the grace of a pachyderm, I skated straight into the set, remembered that I didn't know how to stop, lost my balance, and fell hard on my behind. Our cameramen were on the ball and every movement, every grimace down to the painful thud, was faithfully sent out live to our audiences in western New York, Pennsylvania, and Canada. It was a cute open, so natural and unrehearsed, but I was in real pain. During the show I could barely move from the interview area to the jackpot phone-call set. I found out later that I had actually cracked my tailbone, and it was months before I could sit down without wincing. Ah, yes, let's hear it for resilience!

◆ Hard Work

Work—hard work—is the third ingredient of the P.R.W. factor. No one wants to hear about it, and I don't like to write about it. It's a real drag and certainly won't bring me any popularity votes. We all want to believe there is some easy way to the pot of gold at the end of our rainbows. We're still waiting for the assistant to the prince to arrive with the glass slipper that is a perfect fit, entitling us to the palace, all the ball gowns our hearts desire, and, of course, a life "happily ever after" with the prince! That means no more cleaning the fireplace, no more stubby little brooms blistering those dainty little hands, and no more crabby stepsisters getting on your case.

Well, I waited for that golden coach for thirty-six years and nearly missed the chance to make the most of my life. The prince and his golden coach is that nasty little lie that can linger a lifetime, the fantasy substitute for the reality that we have to *work* for what we get. I would love to tell you that one day I unplugged the vacuum cleaner, changed my clothes, and stepped into the position of television personality. If I had the magic formula that bypassed the hard-work phase, I would be instantly rich and famous. I would also be a charlatan and a liar. The fact is there are no shortcuts! In the past five years I've read nearly fifty best-selling books on success, achievement, and building wealth, from Napoleon Hill's classic, *Think and Grow Rich,* to the current best-seller, *Creating Wealth,* by Robert Allen. Not one author suggests that there is any alternative to hard work.

Without exception the people I've questioned through my career all say that hard work was a major factor in achieving their success.

Sara Eyestone, who traveled all over the country and whose art attracts the extremely wealthy and successful, observes, "I've never met a successful person who does not work hard. You have to pay your dues."

Psychologist Marilyn Machowitz studied sixty early achievers. Among the findings she recently released was that "overnight success is a myth."

Erma Bombeck is a brilliant writer and humorist who has the knack for zeroing in directly on the issue:

"So how come we don't tell them [kids] the truth about work? We have an entire generation of young people growing up who honestly have been told that work must be 'fun, relevant, and meaningful.'"

Whenever I had to do something for which I wasn't prepared, I had to go back and fill in the gap. I spent long afterwork hours "catching up." Whoever said, "Success doesn't come to those who are willing to work only from nine to five," was right.

Barbara Walters left NBC four years before I joined *The Today Show,* but she had become a legend, and stories about her lingered. The one that made the deepest impression on me was about her preparation for covering the investiture of Prince Charles as Prince of Wales. According to one longtime *Today* staffer, Barbara took her secretary to London a week prior to the historic event, and the two of them closeted themselves in a hotel room for the entire week without even going out for meals. Hour after hour Barbara's secretary would place photos of dignitaries and royalty before her. She would then recite their names, titles, complete lineage, history, spouse, relationship to the royal family and the queen. Hundreds of photographs were studied over and over until she got it right. When the cameras rolled on the day of the investiture, Barbara knew that material cold. With confidence she referred in great detail to members of Parliament, foreign dignitaries, and every member of the British royal family who appeared on camera. The NBC control-room staff marveled at her knowledge. The

British were impressed, and our entire nation learned from her informed commentary.

Barbara Walters has become a role model for thousands of women, including me, and she has set a high standard of professionalism for the women and men in television. What few people know is how hard she works, to say nothing of her persistence and resilience, to become who and what she is.

In 1970, Martha Layne Collins was teaching ninth grade in Versailles, Kentucky, population 6,400. She was also raising two children, managing a home, and supporting her husband, who was beginning his dental practice. Today Martha Layne Collins is the governor of Kentucky and a shining example of someone who worked hard to get what she wanted. Raymond Strother, her former media consultant, says it was "tenacity" that got Collins elected. He remarks, "You're looking at Mrs. Housewife who decided she wanted to be governor!"

Martha Layne was a small-town girl who helped set tobacco plants, belonged to the 4-H Club, and was a cheerleader. When she got involved in politics it was as a volunteer. She would bring her children to campaign headquarters, and when it got late and there was still work to be done, she put the kids to sleep in the back room and continued to work. But the real test of her work was the poll that was taken a week after her election. It showed that 32 percent of those who voted for Collins for governor had actually met her, more than three times the average of comparable postelection polls. Year after year, she worked hard at getting out and meeting Kentuckians personally.

Here's another hard work story. This one is close to my heart because it's about a fellow Nebraskan. I grew up knowing that the Nebraska Furniture Mart in Omaha was the *only* place to buy furniture in the state. That is, it was the biggest store with the best prices and the widest selection. The small-town furniture stores just couldn't compete, so people drove from Kansas, Iowa, South Dakota, and from all over Nebraska to visit the Furniture Mart.

Rose Blumkin arrived in the Midwest from Russia in 1917. She was penniless and had to borrow $500 to set up shop in the basement of a pawn shop. It wasn't until 1937, after four children and at the age of forty-three, that she found herself in the furniture business. She had no money for stock, and it seemed that creditors were always pounding on her door. One day, while her children were in school, she sold all the family furniture and appliances to raise money to pay suppliers. Finally she borrowed $50,000 for ninety days from a sympathetic banker. Rose held a sale in a rented hall and made $250,000! Since then she has paid cash for everything. In 1970, she moved the mart to a new location and paid $1.8 million *in cash* for the new building. Now Rose Blumkin is ninety years old. The Nebraska Furniture Mart is the nation's largest furniture store. With the parking lot and warehouses, it covers forty acres. She employs five hundred with an annual payroll of $12 million. This year Mrs. Blumkin expects to do $120 million in sales. Even at the age of ninety, Rose works more than sixty hours a week.

On May 23, 1984, Rose Blumkin was featured on the front page of *The Wall Street Journal*. The headlines read STILL A LIVE WIRE AT 90 . . . A RETAIL PHENOMENON . . . WORK AND LOW PRICES BRING SUCCESS TO ROSE BLUMKIN. The article was prompted by the honor she would receive that day from New York University, the first woman to receive an honorary doctorate in commercial science, a prize the university reserves for "world-class captains of industry."

Rose Blumkin exemplifies everything this book is about. She decided what she wanted. "I used to say, I'm not going to stay in this basement forever. Someday I'm gonna have a good-looking store. . . ." And she does. Rose Blumkin's life could serve to illustrate any chapter in this book, but I chose to place her in the hard-work category. It's easy to think of all the advantages and the recognition millionaires get, but for her millions Rose worked hard, long hours seven days a week for sixty years!

More than anything else, it's the work of life that gives us a feeling of purpose and dignity, that makes us feel fully human and proud.

◆◆

What is your P.R.W. factor?

P = Persistence
- PERSIST—Stick with your goal no matter how long it may take.
- PERSIST—Every day can't be a red-letter day. Keep going even though the work may seem tedious and unrewarding.
- PERSIST—When others say you can't, prove that you can!

R = Resilience
- Don't be upset by negative comments and criticism.
- Set your own standards, and strive to meet them. Ignore outside distractions.
- If setbacks and negative criticism leave you hurting, bounce back! Pick yourself up, brush yourself off, and get back in the game.

W = Work
- Push up your sleeves and dig in. Your goal is worth working for.
- Expect long hours, sore muscles, and mental fatigue.
- Don't waste time looking for shortcuts. Pay your dues.

◆◆

Use the P.R.W. factor to get to your goals. It works! It's worth it. You will have the satisfaction of a job well done and rewards well deserved.

7

◆

Comic Relief

*Humor can make disasters
less devastating, tension more tolerable,
and bad days more bearable.*
—JEANNIE RALSTON

ANYONE's PLIGHT CAN be lightened with humor. It's really the only thing that works for me during those times when I feel the whole world is against me, when nothing seems to be going right and I feel like the only one who ever suffered these latest abuses. Lots of people thought that the life of a homemaker was a continuous vacation until humorist Erma Bombeck set the record straight, with humor. Millions of women who felt misunderstood, exploited, overworked, and underappreciated flock to Erma's column each day for a giggle that sustains them through the "valley of motherhood." In the evenings millions of husbands would sit through an oral reading of an Erma column dealing with a subject close to home. It provides a nonthreatening way to say, "See how it is here! This is what I have to put up with." Erma Bombeck has become a soul mate and a master of saying, "I understand what you're going through, and here's how we can deal with it." Her efforts were finally recognized by serious journalists, and she appeared on the cover of *Time* on July 2, 1984.

Even before the *Cincinnati Enquirer* began carrying Erma's daily column I depended on making light of my frustrations by finding friends who were also stuck at home with preschoolers, one family car (which you only had two days a week), and no cleaning woman. Miniskirts were the rage during those young homemaker years when we lived in the smallest house in an upscale subdivision. I can remember joking with a friend after attending a particularly elegant neighborhood party. "Well, I was the only one at the party who didn't have a cleaning woman."

"How could you tell?"

"I was the only woman there with bruised knees from removing wax buildup!"

One particularly rough day I ran to the pediatrician, delivered cupcakes to nursery school, prepared for a birthday, emptied the mousetraps, dealt with a repairman who had come to fix the driveway, and had the dishwasher break down—all before noon! Finally, I fed the kids, put Billy down for his nap, and asked Jeff and two neighbor boys to play quietly in the sandbox while I rested. Then I filled the tub up to the top with American Beauty Rose bubble bath and put a purple "revitalizing masque" on my face. Just as I settled back for some relaxation, the door to the bathroom flew open and Jeff, along with four little boys, crowded around the tub, staring. "Mom, Tommy and Joey want to play, too. We need more spoons, and do we have another muffin tin to make igloo villages?" I couldn't decide whether to cry or be angry. So I drew a little cartoon in my head and laughed.

A couple of weeks later my husband called from the office to say that he would like to bring one of his account people home for dinner. I had been refinishing furniture all day. The house was a mess, and I was a mess. There were empty potato-chip sacks, Popsicle sticks, and apple cores all over the family room. The boys had made Kool-Aid, and there was sugar on the counter and crunching underfoot. They had also fixed cereal, peanut butter and crackers, and bacon. We went to plan B.

The boys took a garbage bag around and picked up the house. I took lasagna out of the freezer and ran to the store for French bread. I used nail-polish remover to get the furniture stain from under my nails and jumped into the shower to remove the grime of the day spent in my self-made furniture repair shop. I hadn't even finished getting soaped up when the jet of water fizzled to a drip, then stopped. Of all times for the cistern to run dry! Bill was due home with our dinner guest at any moment; it began to pour outside, and I decided it would serve him right if they rounded the lane and found me in the front yard blithely rinsing off under nature's shower. Of course, if they were late, the neighbors would witness the scene first and probably have me carted off to the police station. So I wiped myself off with Wet Ones and suffered through the evening feeling sticky and smelling medicinal. But the picture of myself standing stark naked in the rain with bath brush and shaver helped me smile in the face of adversity and no water. Humor helps us see the absurdities of life, and this was absurd!

American humor seems to specialize in making light of life's hardships. Without a sense of humor I could never have survived motherhood, moving twelve times, divorce, the television business, or, for that matter, writing this book! It's our tradition as Americans to confront adversity with a grin and a chuckle.

People drive for miles to see a funny act. Our good comedians become celebrities and movie stars. We honor them for their ability to help us see the funny side of life and that lightens the load. We've all experienced the glorious release after a couple of hours of laughing until our stomachs hurt and the tears roll. We've all experienced the unexplained, uncontrollable giggles that attack us at the most inopportune times, like in a class, at church, or during a concert.

Recently, professionals have begun to take humor seriously. Psychologists, sociologists, physicians, and journalists have begun to accept humor as a subject worthy of study. Three world conferences have been held on humor. College courses are being offered on it. The role of humor in American politics has been debated. Humor is being touted as a healer, stress reliever, internal exerciser, sleep inducer, almost everything but simple entertainer. W. C. Fields, who probably knew the most about it, observed, "You never know why people laugh. I know *what* makes them laugh, but trying to get your hands on the *why* of it is like trying to pick an eel out of a tub of water."

Many doctors are prescribing laughter to relieve physical and mental illness, and as preventive therapy. Psychiatrists agree that one of the first signs of mental illness is the loss of the sense of humor, and conversely, its return is one of the early signs of recovery.

Dr. William Fry, Jr., associate clinical professor of psychiatry at Stanford University, found hearty, really rolling-in-the-aisles laughter to be good exercise, a kind of "stationary jogging." Researchers found that the blood pressure rises and the pulse rate can double during a good laugh.

Norman Cousins's experience with laughter as a healer and a pain reliever has gained worldwide attention and given more credence to the notion of laughter as therapy. In his book *Anatomy of an Illness,* Cousins reports how he overcame a degenerative spinal condition by watching classic comic films and television programs and reading funny books. Cousins writes, "What was significant about the laughter . . . [was] that it creates a mood in which the positive emotions can be put to work. . . . In short, it helps make it possible for good things to happen."

Health magazine reported on a Los Angeles convalescent home that brought in a comedian to entertain patients. There was a general psychological and physiological improvement.

Traditionally, there haven't been many laughs in corporate America, for those buttoned-down, buttoned-up Harvard MBAs take themselves, their jobs, and the *universe* very seriously. However, even big business has softened toward humor. In February 1982, *The Wall Street Journal* listed four ways to avoid psychological fatigue. Number two was, "Keep your sense of humor. . . . An able business leader knows how to help his group discharge their tension by injecting an appropriate note of levity. . . . It does seem to relieve stress and release constructive energies."

That more receptive attitude toward chuckles in the boardroom opened the door for Bob Basso and his Completely

Outrageous Workshops (COW). Basso, an actor and drama coach, devised a three-hour session in "laughter therapy." He stumbled onto the technique while teaching comedy workshops in Los Angeles. "I realized that laughter, coupled with game playing, was a great coping mechanism." For his sessions, which are usually conducted in conference rooms or hotel meeting rooms, Basso draws from his repertoire of two hundred tension-relieving games. His theme is, "Don't be so full of the adult that there is no room for the child in you."

Basso has sober executives dress up in girdles and silly hats, drawing pictures of people they don't like and mostly laughing while sharpening their skills in play. New York Life Insurance and the IRS are among his corporate clients; to me, it's comforting to know that there are major organizations practicing a survival mechanism I have used for a long time.

Perhaps the "trickle-down effect" didn't have much impact on the economy, but the humor from the nation's highest office did trickle down. Our nation has been blessed with several presidents who have set a high standard of using wit with style to diffuse criticism and reduce anxiety. John F. Kennedy's humor has been widely praised and carefully recorded for history. One of his most memorable remarks came just after he appointed his brother Robert as attorney general. Many people don't realize that presidents, like comedians, hire comedy writers to help them prepare for these occasions when humor and zingy one-liners are needed. In his book *Live Longer Through Laughter,* Joey Adams takes credit for President Kennedy's response to the uproar over Bobby's appointment. When asked, "How could you appoint a young boy, and your brother, as attorney general?" the president looked down and smiled. "Well, he's my kid brother, and I wanted to give him some experience before he opened his own law office." It was masterly.

When the whole nation was in shock over the attempted assassination of President Reagan, he put everyone at ease with his first words after emergency surgery. "I'm sorry, Nancy, I forgot to duck."

Although it's fortunate to have a president who sets such an exemplary standard of using humor in the face of adversity, I needed no presidential mandate to look for comic relief during my daily foibles on *A.M. Buffalo*. It was fortunate that my co-host had a marvelous sense of humor. He sparked my own wit and together we got through some pretty hopeless situations. Each day we dragged in, got a cup of coffee from the machine, looked over the show's format, and started with one-liners to get our energy level up, put a sparkle in our eyes, and pump up our level of enthusiasm for making compost, preventing senility, making a meal from a single turnip, sewing a complete wardrobe from one bed sheet, and discussing the other hot topics on the show that day.

Because I was less experienced, and scared, Brian tended to be the dominant host. As I gained confidence and ability, I really had to assert myself to assume a more equal role. I used playful humor to give myself an entry in the rapid-fire conversations. The pattern had developed that at the top of the show Brian would launch into a narrative about something that had happened to him, perhaps give his impression or opinion of something, which left me little room for comment. I decided that something had to be done. The next morning as the theme music came up and the floor director was on the final countdown, "ten . . . nine . . .", I looked down at Brian's lap and said, "Hurry, Brian, your fly is unzipped!" The timing was perfect. The red light of the camera came on just as Brian was looking down at his crotch, reaching for his zipper. Another time the second before the camera came on, I asked him if he realized that he was wearing one brown sock and one black one. At home the viewers saw the opening shot of Brian holding his feet up to the light to see if his socks matched, while I said, "Good morning. I'm Nancy Foreman, welcome to *A.M. Buffalo*. Once this gentleman next to me gets his shoes on the right feet, we can start off with a jackpot phone call." I knew Brian would take my humor as it was meant, just a playful "Gotcha!" Believe me, he got his "gotchas," too. It made our work more lively and fun, and while we made each other laugh we developed a deep respect for one another which showed in our on-air teamwork. The ailing morning program we took over had become the most successful locally produced program in the nation by the time I left Buffalo to accept a position on *Today*.

It would be impossible to consider the importance of humor in our lives without mentioning Willard Scott, *Today's* off-the-wall weatherman. For my first two and a half years on *Today,* I had an office adjoining Willard's. There was *never* a dull moment. Willard not only uses humor to get his energy level up, he uses it to make others laugh and feel good. He is a genuinely funny man whose humor has become a part of his real personality. The real Willard is an imposing six-foot-four three-hundred-pounder with a jovial, booming voice. It never fails to crack up the entire cast and crew when Willard enters the studio and grabs the short, bald audio man and gives him a loud, smacking kiss on the top of his shiny head. It helps to ease the tension of network news and lighten the very nature of morning network television, the inflexible sec ond hand, and the pressure of an unforgiving camera.

Willard is the first to admit how important humor is to him professionally. He tells about the time he was asked to anchor the annual Christmas service broadcast at the National Cathedral in Washington. This was a straight anchor assignment and not exactly an occasion for crazy hats or funny repartee with the clergy. He describes his symptoms during the broadcast: "I started to perspire, my hands shook, my voice got higher, and I was losing it! I realized that I feel most confident in situations where I can use humor. Maybe it's a kind of professional crutch." Since then, Willard has consciously avoided the somber assignments, and he sticks to what he likes best, being funny.

While we're talking about *The Today Show,* I should mention what a blow it was for me to move from Buffalo, where I was a local celebrity, to an environment that was accustomed to hosting world leaders, award-winning athletes, and Hollywood stars. I thought that landing the job would mean that I was a pretty formidable television talent. Instead I was met with a "who are *you?*" attitude, which was really more devastating than hostility. The indifference was a blow that only humor could soothe. In my previous professional assignments, whether I was good, bad, or mediocre, my colleagues and producers had always been interested in me and my professional progress. At NBC I didn't have the independence, the recognition, or the power. And the seven-minute capsule tape of my Buffalo work that was instrumental in landing the network assignment was only seen by a couple of producers. Even that tape could hardly express the two years of consistently serving a television market with love and commitment. So I found myself in the famous Studio 8G at 30 Rockefeller Plaza in the very heart of Manhattan, a complete nobody! Yes, it was the right decision. Yes, I was happy that I had achieved my goal; but I must admit that my sense of humor worked overtime for a while.

The interviews that I worked so hard preparing didn't get as much attention as the commercials I did. I remember one week I was especially proud of an interview I conducted with a woman who wrote a book on grief management, or how to handle the loss of a loved one. Granted it's a dark subject, but she offered sound advice, added new information to a traditionally hush-hush subject, and I considered it a real breakthrough to get the producers to bring her on. On the same day I did the interview I had done a commercial for Alpo dog food. Later that day I was still feeling a sense of pride and accomplishment over my interview, so I was delighted when a stranger came up to me and said, "What a great job you do. I really enjoyed seeing you on TV today, and that dog was so adorable!" It took a moment to figure out that she was referring to the commercial and not my breakthrough interview. I had a good laugh. "Here I am on the big NBC network, and it's the dog they remember!"

I depended on my humor to soothe the occasional sting to my ego caused from no longer being a "star." I had grown accustomed to being a local celebrity, and on *Today,* the only woman broadly recognized is Jane Pauley. The first few times I arrived on location to do a videotaped interview, I found that the guests were expecting Jane. I understand how that happens. One person says that Nancy Foreman from *The Today Show* is coming to do an interview, then the next person can't remember the name, so it's some woman from *The Today Show,* and the next person assumes that if it's a woman on *The Today Show,* it must be Jane Pauley. Last summer I was in Wilmington, Delaware, doing a story, and a woman came up to me and said, "Jane, you look so different in person!" And people still slow down as they drive by my mother's home in Lakeland, Florida. She often sees them point and say, "That's where Jane Pauley's mother lives." She loves it.

Unfortunately, too many successful high achievers lose perspective, and their goals become obsessions magnified into life-or-death, do-or-die ultimatums. You have seen them, with their iron-jawed, hollow-eyed, glum faces, trudging diligently to the next goal. Somehow in the course of their journey they've lost sight of the experience of *living;* everything has become a form of competition. The truth is the journey itself is as important as the goal. How you get there is as important as getting there. In her book *Go for It,* Dr. Irene Kassorla says it eloquently: "All any of us have is now, our todays. Everyone you know is dying; no one gets out of this beautiful world alive. The "win" in life is enjoying every precious moment. . . ." Humor makes the whole adventure more enjoyable. It sharpens the mind, reminds us of our own frailties, and helps us to be more tolerant of others. Humor soothes a wounded ego, it relieves not only tension but boredom, it relaxes, it opens up communication, it invites friendship and warmth, and it has a positive effect on our health and fitness.

As an experiment, the patients being discharged from a Los Angeles Veterans Administration Hospital were given this prescription: "Laughter to be experienced for fifteen minutes per day." Unless I attend a funny movie or play, I seldom sustain laughter for fifteen minutes; however, I do adhere to the advice "A laugh a day keeps the shrink away."

For many people it may not be that easy to just turn on the laughter. It grows out of a different way of looking at life, like slipping a different lens on life's camera to get another view. It may take extra effort in the beginning, but developing a sense of humor, looking for the comedy in life, is one of the most valuable success components anyone can carry through life.

Let humor transform frustration into a funny scene instead of an angry one. Let laughter relieve fear. *Today's* weatherman, Willard Scott, is a master at turning mistakes into funny lines and sour guests into delightful, entertaining company. When I am bothered by stage fright, I know that a few laughs with Willard will relax me and calm my nerves.

◆ *Humor to the Rescue!*

One of my least favorite pickles is being stuck in traffic. The other one is when my camera crew is called off my assignment and sent to a higher-priority news story. Getting angry or frustrated is a waste. Instead, I dream up lines that would turn the scene into a comedy, and if there is no funny inspiration, I think what Steve Martin or Rich Little would say or do in my situation. It usually works!

The push for a higher goal or a change of position takes extra effort and energy. You have to work harder and longer, take more risks, adjust to change. The same traits that make you a high achiever are also the most stressful. Humor helps diffuse the pressure and restore equilibrium. Humor also improves the quality of life and makes the climb to success much more enjoyable.

How about a hearty laugh at least once a day? Here are some ways to get the laugh machine working:

1. Remind yourself each morning that you will find something humorous about yourself or an incident that occurs to you during the day. Make a sign or symbol as a reminder to think funny. Tape it to the bathroom mirror, stick it to a credit card, attach it to your dashboard, the phone, anywhere you'll be sure to see it.

2. Under no circumstances should humor be used at the expense of another. While I preach the gospel of humor, it can also be cruel and destructive; humor can be used to malign, belittle, and demoralize. Sadly, when humor is in that way abused, it reflects more powerfully upon the character and the quality of the person who is dispensing the venom than it does upon the victim. A confident, secure person laughs at himself and his plight, not others.

3. Get the laugh machinery moving. Buy a funny book or record. It can be whimsical, like Peanuts or Garfield, or it might be a collection of your favorite one-liners or a come-

dian's stand-up routines. Keep the book or record handy when you need a laugh.

4. Who's your favorite cartoon character? If you don't have one, adopt one. Start clipping cartoons from newspapers and magazines that you find especially funny or in sync with your particular situation. Tape them to your office door or to the refrigerator. Frame the classics on your wall.

5. Keep a card file of jokes or stories that make you laugh. As your file grows you can begin to categorize or color code your material. Then during the down times you have a place to turn for solace and laughter. If you are facing a tough day, pull a joke from your file that you can share with a friend, or save it for a private chuckle.

6. Does your town have Dial-a-Joke? If so, get in the habit of checking in for the new joke each day.

7. If you own a videotape recorder, rent or purchase movies that make you laugh out loud. Give in to it . . . and feel the catharsis.

8. Sharpen your imagination. Begin to adopt your own brand of humor. Learn to draw your own mental cartoons. Develop your own one-liners. Remember, corporate heads, politicians, lecturers, even presidents find fitting jokes and occasionally hire writers for needed one-liners, which they carefully rehearse to sound spontaneous and natural. It makes everybody happy.

9. Learn to step outside yourself. Try to see yourself as an actor in a movie . . . from the audience's point of view. Be playful and inventive in your imaginary performance.

As humorist Robert S. Weider says, "Humor bridges the gap between the perfections we seek and the imperfections we're stuck with." And when Charlie Chaplin was asked, "What is humor?" he replied, "It is a kind of gentle and benevolent custodian of the mind, which prevents us from being overwhelmed by the apparent 'seriousness of life.' "

Bring more laughter into your life. You will have more fun on your way to success, and so will those around you.

◆◆

Here's what laughter can do:
- Relieve stress.
- Provide good physical exercise.
- Prevent us from taking ourselves too seriously.
- Restore perspective.
- Make adversity more bearable.
- Attract friends.
- Transform negative emotions into positive feelings.
- Be enjoyed alone or in a crowd.
- Be a universal language.
- Feel good! It's a positive emotion.

◆◆

8

◆

Have Faith in Failure

---

*Being licked is
valuable if we are to learn from it.*
—DR. DAVID SCHWARTZ

THERE WERE FIFTY-TWO seniors in my high school graduating class. Albion High School never invited a visiting commencement speaker. It had been the tradition to select the top three speech students to deliver the commencement speeches. I was thrilled to be named a graduation speaker. My speech was quite predictable—full of all the clichés, uplifting quotations, and references to school, family, community, God, and country. Since the speakers were named early in the year, it gave us plenty of time to prepare, maybe too much. Since it was the most important speech of the year, a speech that would be heard by half the town, the speech teacher made sure the grammar and usage were correct. We each delivered our speeches several times privately for him, and we each received his coaching to polish our delivery and style while at the same time becoming more comfortable and confident.

I had tried using notes on index cards, but I decided to stick with the complete text. There was reason to be nervous, but I was well prepared. I could give that speech in my sleep! Stage fright had never been a problem for me. Although "butterflies" were a common affliction before any kind of performance, I had from the age of six appeared before groups on many occasions, and I had learned to handle almost any audience situation without difficulty. But the graduation speech was a big deal at a time in life when even getting a haircut or a new shade of lipstick was a big deal.

Congregated in the high school gymnasium were all my classmates, all the teachers, the entire student body, all my relatives and immediate family, and probably half of Albion. I got halfway through my speech and simply stopped. My mind went blank, and nothing would come out of my mouth. I had prepared for this eventuality and had my entire speech in front of me. But that didn't help. I became so flustered and confused that I couldn't even remember where I'd left off. This had been my worst fear, and it was actually happening! I wanted to die. The audience shuffled and coughed. My steady boyfriend looked down and blushed. I'm sure that my parents were writhing in embarrassment, too.

There was a long silence. I frankly don't remember how I signed off and returned to my seat. The mayor had been standing in the wings waiting to hand out the diplomas. Afterward, he rushed over to me and said, "I felt so terrible for you. I wanted to come out there and help you find your place." I was crushed; I didn't feel like attending any of the graduation parties, even the family get-together that my parents had arranged. I just wanted to go quietly to a remote cornfield and expire.

It was a devastating public failure—particularly because I had always considered public speaking to be one of my strongest skills. I vowed never to speak in public again. I would simply become a nurse or a missionary.

But since speech was a required subject in my first college semester, I found myself back in the same work saddle. Much to my surprise, I was doing very well. I was more relaxed about speaking to groups. I wasn't as tense during the preparation, and I felt more confident in trying out new material. My interpretive reading gained the recognition of the head of the department, and I was selected to represent Nebraska at several collegiate speech contests. I was doing what I thought I could never do again—and doing it better!

Failing miserably, suffering public embarrassment, and living through it brings a special brand of liberation. What I had feared most had in fact happened, and I survived. Afterward there had been some terribly uncomfortable hours and days, and I had cried myself to sleep for several nights, but the sun continued to rise, my family continued to love me, and the Omaha *World Herald* continued to appear at the door each morning.

As I gravitated toward speech as a college major, I wondered why I seemed to be doing so well in the very course of study that required skills that had failed me so miserably. I figured out that first, there had been too much time for preparation, and I had probably overprepared. I'd had the speech memorized word for word at least two months before graduation. Second, I had programmed my own failure by visualizing the worst that could happen over and over in vivid detail. It became a self-fulfilling prophecy. Finally, I didn't trust being too successful. Unconsciously I was afraid that if I became outstanding, I would not be popular.

◆ *The Lessons of Failure*

For the first time I realized that failure could offer valuable lessons, actually help me perform better. My conversations with some of America's leading high achievers have confirmed this solid truth: If you are to be successful, failure is unavoidable. Seize the opportunity to learn from your mistakes. There are no substitutes for the lessons learned from failure.

As Dr. Irene Kassorla writes in *Go for It:* "Winners make friends with failure. Failures offer valuable information about where not to go next time, and are helpful guides, not signals to give up." She explains that failure is a part of the success pattern. No one achieves their goals in one straight climb. It is a jagged, uneven ascent with curves and plateaus, but it does move up! In his best-seller *Creating Wealth,* Robert Allen quotes Herb True: "Successful people often have more failures than failures do. But they keep going." And

Robert Allen, who built an empire in real estate, says, "One good failure can teach you more about success than four years at the best university. Failure is the best thing that ever happened to you."

In *The Magic of Thinking Big,* Dr. David Schwartz tells what he discovered about failure from talking to the social workers and law enforcement people who had regular contact with the down-and-out, the outcasts of society found huddled on park benches or in the gutters of most urban areas. We have all seen them and cringed. These are the ruined, defeated, bottomed-out people of the world. Men and women, young and old, some highly educated, some not—all conquered by one of life's many blows. It's astonishing that their stories are not significantly different from those of the very successful, but in each case the street people's stories ended with the big adversity. "I lost my job and my wife." "I lost everything in a bad business venture with my best friend." Another reports, "My husband became ill, and we were wiped out." The very same themes of hardship turn up in the stories of high achievers, but they learn from failures and go on with more experience, better insights, more information, and keener intuition.

◆ Good-bye Failure—Hello Setback

The difference between the down-and-out and those on top is the way they perceive failure. To those who sleep in public restrooms and on park benches, a failure did mean the end of their world. The sun didn't continue to shine in their minds. They interpreted one of life's catastrophes as a kind of personal annihilation and allowed it to totally destroy their sense of self, of purpose, and of relationships.

The high achiever is able to accept failure as a temporary setback and use that experience to improve his or her performance. Failures can be the most valuable lessons, not just in a particular business, but in life. Over and over I hear declarations like "Getting fired was the best thing that ever happened to me," and "The divorce, although a terrible blow, forced me to grow up, and now I'm a better person. My present marriage is healthy."

No one sets out to fail. It's something we dread and make

every effort to avoid. But if we are to succeed, we have to take risks, try new opportunities, and that brings some inevitable failures. As Dr. David Schwartz confirms, "It is not possible to win high-level success without meeting opposition, hardship, and setback. But it is possible to use setbacks to propel you forward."

I certainly have had more than one failure in life, and with each one I grew stronger, more determined, and gained something new from each one. One failure that was particularly difficult occurred during my first brush with live television. At KOLN-TV in Lincoln, Nebraska, when I was co-hosting *The Joe Martin Show,* I was asked to take over the live commercial for a major bank. The regular staff announcer, a handsome devil with a voice that could move mountains, was going on vacation; I was to substitute. At the time I was the reigning Miss Nebraska, a college senior engaged to a graduate business major. I was doing well in my college work, and although working from ten P.M. to midnight was difficult, I really didn't have a demanding role on *The Joe Martin Show,* so I felt confident that I could handle the commercials.

In 1961 television commercials were one minute long. That's an eternity compared to the ten-, twenty-, and thirty-second spots we have today. Also, at that time there was no teleprompter, or if there was one, I didn't know about it. So I had to memorize one minute of difficult copy that had to be delivered rapidly and with authority. I had absolutely no understanding of interest rates, minimum deposits, or federally insured accounts, and I could not have cared less about the crazy hours their banks were open. So for me it was like trying to memorize sixty seconds of a foreign language, smiling all the time and pointing to a large poster at the right moment. Well, it was a disaster. For the first two nights I ruined the entire commercial. Then a sympathetic prop man offered to make me cue cards. That made it worse, for I kept looking from the camera to the card, squinting, losing my place in the card. Since I made an extra fifteen dollars for the bank commercials, I kept up the futile effort for nearly a month.

It's one thing to mess up a speech, but the commercial

copy demanded an articulate review of complicated percentages, dividends, branch locations, and customer hours. While the station would be irritated if I misread the copy, the SEC takes an even dimmer view of misrepresenting financial information. Things went from bad to worse. My performance deteriorated because of my anxiety and my acute awareness that I was failing as a live commercial spokesperson. Finally the call came from the account executive who was handling the advertising campaign for the bank. She suggested that we "have coffee and talk a bit." She could not have fired me more gently. In fact, it took a couple of hours to realize that I had, in fact, been fired. Frankly, I don't know why they let me muddle through as long as they did.

That failure became another valuable lesson. When years later in Buffalo the opportunity to do live commercials presented itself once again, I drew on the experience to correct my earlier difficulties. I changed my pattern of preparation. I used simulation by setting up a camera with props and going through the movements; instead of visualizing the worst, I imagined myself performing perfectly. Then I learned to relax and look as if I were enjoying the message, and soon I really was! On *Today* I am required to handle a broad range of commercial clients, from conservative AT&T and American Express, to the unpredictable Alpo dog food, complete with a veritable menagerie of live dogs, props, and pans of dog food. I still continue to prepare just as carefully as I did when I was a novice. I remember one day Billy came home from school to find that I had stacked all the towels on the dining room table to rehearse a tricky move replacing several towels exactly on top of another stack without looking. It had to be felt while smiling and bubbling, "Colorful, washable, fashionable. Cotton performs." I'm no longer paralyzed with the fear that I'll blow it. I know how that feels: not good. But thanks to a couple of nasty failures, I know how to avoid making the mistakes that can sabotage my pursuit toward high goals.

◆ *Failures Don't Hide*

One of the problems with failure is that it is a social taboo.

We don't like to discuss failure, we don't even like to read or hear about it. It is uncomfortable to know about the failure of someone we know because we automatically think, "Oh, no, that could be me." Like death, failure is a hush-hush subject at cocktail parties and business meetings. No wonder we don't know how to handle it, let alone accept it as a stepping-stone to success. We are conditioned, in fact expected to become successful, but no one tells us that we must encounter failure. No one tells us how to turn failure into strength. As family therapist Virginia Satir declares, "Every person has the right to fail."

Why aren't we more honest about failure? Why is it that we deny our shortcomings and inadequacies? In the struggle to build self-esteem in our children, perhaps we have gone overboard in protecting them from failures. I have been just as guilty as other parents in accepting shoddy behavior, grades, and work from kids who can do better. I can hear myself saying, "You did a beautiful job making your bed," when, in fact, a monkey could have done a better job. Or, "Don't feel bad that you struck out again; you really held the bat so well." Sometimes we should be able to say, "I know it doesn't feel good to strike out. Let's figure out what we can do to improve."

In 1977, Fredelle Maynard wrote an article for *Woman's Day* magazine about turning failure into success. She wisely states, "The trouble with failure-prevention devices is that they leave a child unequipped for life in the real world. . . . Parents should not offer a quick consolation prize or say 'It doesn't matter,' because it does. The youngster should be allowed to experience disappointment and then be helped to master it."

Most of us are adults before we confront failure. David Elias is an exception. David is a successful independent financial adviser with offices in Buffalo and New York's posh Olympic Tower on Fifth Avenue. He is a regular financial contributor for *Town & Country* magazine and the investment editor for *Physicians' Investment Journal*. This year David's company is expanding its services to European clients. Among his clients are several gorgeous top New York models whose incomes soar into the higher six figures. He was recently my guest on *Today,* and afterward I had an opportunity to talk to him about how he achieved his financial and professional goals. David attributed much of his success and knowledge of business to his understanding of failure.

From early childhood, David suffered from a serious speech problem; he stuttered badly and later it was found that he also had dyslexia. He did not have the good fortune to be surrounded by an enlightened support group. His teachers called him stupid, his guidance counselor called him a bum, and his classmates called him a loser. His grades dropped, he became a difficult behavior problem, and he was expelled from school several times. His parents had all but given up. Out of desperation, David's father put him to work cleaning toilets in the school on Saturdays. He said, "David, this is what your life will be like if you continue to fail." That was the turning point for David. He was a tenth-grader and at the end of the year he asked to repeat the grade. He asked for another failure, on his terms, because he knew that he had missed some valuable lessons. He began to turn failure into success. He organized a lawn-mowing service for his neighbors in Geneva, New York. He became so successful that he hired several friends to mow while he handled marketing, public relations, and sales. At the same time, David was also running a double paper route, and on Saturdays he delivered milk. Most of his earnings went to pay for speech therapy and remedial-reading lessons. With any extra money he bought stock in AT&T, which he later used for his college expenses. The proudest moment of his young life was when he received the V.F.W. Citizen of the Year award and delivered a speech without stumbling to fifteen thousand people. Now, in his midthirties, David freely talks about the many times he had to dig out of failures. By all standards, David is a success, but he knows that setbacks are unavoidable, and what is more important, he knows how to turn them around.

Unfortunately, there is no substitute for failure. There is no way to learn about it through study and research. Business students can read volumes of case studies and become experts in understanding business failures, but there is no way to know what it feels like unless you experience it for yourself. It would be like trying to describe what it's like to have a baby or how it feels to parachute or scuba-dive. You can read the books, see the instructional films, interview experts on the subject, but until you actually experience the labor pains, the rush of air as you jump from a plane, or the haunting silence of the ocean depths, you cannot really know the feeling, and that visceral information is just as valuable, sometimes more valuable, than any hard data.

◆ Don't Blame Others

In *The Magic of Thinking Big,* David Schwartz wrote, "We're quick to accept full credit for our victories . . . but human beings are equally quick to blame someone else for each setback."

So many people use the scapegoat method of dealing with failure. If the manager doesn't make the quota, it is the fault of the salesman. The salesman blames the slow holiday season, or the competitor's product, or the car that breaks down. If the home team doesn't win, it's so easy to blame the coach, the field conditions, player injury, or poor officials. There is no way to learn from failure if we refuse to take responsibility for our own shortcomings.

My particular failures offered an advantage. I simply couldn't pass the blame on to someone else. I had no choice. There I was, all by myself for all to see. The camera was working fine. Everything was working but me. I had to take responsibility for the problem.

Remember the skid-row dropouts. They blamed their plight on everything but themselves. Something always caused their demise—cast them into a life of misery, poverty, and self-pity. High achievers accept their mistakes and failures, learn from them, and go on.

◆ Don't Blame It on Luck

Another popular method of dealing with failure is a superficial "disconnection." Just think how many times you've heard a hard-luck story capped with "Well, that's the way the ball bounces," or "That's the way the cookie crumbles," as if there's some vague outside force spinning scenarios of adversity that we can't do anything about. We are supposed to accept them with respectful resignation as a part of life. And that teaches us nothing. It simply reinforces the belief in bad luck and "destiny." My grandmother used to say, "It's just one of those things." That certainly put an end to my questions. And I learned nothing. Until you can say, "I performed badly," or "I really messed up," there is no way to get to the constructive learning failure can bring.

◆ *Time Out*

Failure can heave a nasty blow—it can really undermine your confidence. Take some time to regroup and get your bearings. Give yourself a "cooling off" period to get some emotional distance. The tears and dust must settle before any clear assessment can be made. That's the period when I find great solace in saying, "It could have been worse." Much like after a fender-bender, you must first congratulate yourself that no one was hurt before you start thinking about what it may cost to have the front end repaired.

The length of time you require will vary. A major business collapse may require six months or more, but a minor career setback like not getting a raise or a promotion may only take a week or two. Soon you will rediscover that the world is still turning right on schedule.

◆ *Rewind—Replay*

In television we can replay the videotapes to find the weak spots and problems. In the screening room we stop the tape, rewind it, and take another look. There they are in living color—all the mistakes! We call it "postproduction." It's a rehashing, finding the problems and coming up with solutions.

Try holding a postproduction meeting with yourself. Be the executive producer of your own failure. Ask yourself what happened and why. Or compare your failure to the defective engine of a car, and tear it apart. Be the mechanic. Break down the failure into its basic components, lay them out like parts or blocks, analyze each part, find the weak ones, the faulty ones. Then run some tests, make substitutions and adjustments. Correct ineffective methods or procedures. Find your mistakes, and fix them!

In the case of my first miserable failed television commercial I had a whole list of mistakes to correct. First, I had misjudged the work. I had assumed that all I had to do was read over a one-minute bank commercial, smile, and somehow everything would happen as it did in class when I presented a dramatic reading. I had not considered the conditions of the television studio with the hot lights, the cameras, the distractions of the behind-the-camera activities of the floor crew. I expected people to stop and listen to me, to look at me. Instead, there were no people, no faces, no audience. I couldn't even see the face of the camera operator, and it took some time to understand that he could see me! I had seen others deliver commercials, and it looked so easy that I mistakenly assumed it was. I had wrongly believed that if I could effectively deliver a speech or reading in a college course, I could deliver any style of copy regardless of the content. I thought that a simple walk to the sign and a gesture toward some numbers would feel natural at the designated time. Oh, I had a lot to fix! But by breaking down the complete situation, not just the copy, I was able to find even the hidden problems.

◆ *How to Fix Failures*

VISUALIZE YOUR BEST—NOT YOUR WORST

In the chapter on visualization I discussed some of the incredible powers of the imagination and how to use them to your advantage in achieving goals. The down side of visualization is that the same mechanism can just as effectively program failure, defeat, humiliation, all the things we want to avoid. By thinking about them, and imagining them in living color with all the emotional side effects—feeling nervous, dreading the moment, sweaty palms—we are, in fact, arranging for the reality. That was a major cause of my own failure. My visualization was unintentionally undermining my ability to really learn my new assignment. Before each commercial, my dread of failing again became a mental scenario worst than the last.

It is important to examine failures, to see where we went wrong, to understand our misjudgments; but it is just as important to move on. Don't dwell on the problems and failures once the lessons have had an impact, for if you overanalyze or become too captivated by your own failings, analysis paralysis sets in and instead of growing you get stuck in a rut. In fact, you can become preoccupied with defeat to the point of causing it.

In Psycho-Cybernetics, Dr. Maxwell Maltz explains further:

> As soon as the error has been recognized as such, and the correction of course made, it is equally important that the error be consciously forgotten. . . . If we consciously dwell upon the error, or consciously feel guilty about the error, and keep berating ourselves because of it, then unwittingly the error or failure becomes the "goal". . . .

Once you are satisfied that you understand what went wrong, and you have figured out the new approach, get the failure out of your mind.

NONSTICK FAILURE

When I quizzed high achievers about their failures I constantly got the same reaction—a puzzled look, a pause, and then the question "You mean were there bad times?" Once I changed the word "failure" to "setbacks" or "rough going," the most amazing tales of loss and defeat would tumble out. But they did not consider any of them personal failures. For high achievers failure just doesn't compute as devastation, defeat, the end of the world.

When I blew the graduation speech or got fired from the KOLN-TV commercial assignment, I did not internalize the problem as personal failure. Although discouraging and disappointing, those experiences were no reflection on me as a person. I knew that whatever happened I could try again, move on to something else, consider new options. Like other achievers, I have never considered myself a failure. Heaven knows that I've faced adversity and suffered setbacks, but they entered my perception as just that: temporary setbacks, the kind everyone has. My brain does not compute failure.

You may have heard Sally Raphael on late-night radio. Sally Jessy Raphael started out in small-town radio, then moved to local television in St. Louis, and is now the host of *Talknet*, NBC's nationally syndicated nighttime radio call-in talk show. Sally J. Raphael is currently negotiating for a pay raise that will put her in the six figures and for a syndicated television talk show that could make her a household name. The person behind the name and the success has suffered incredible failures during her twenty years in broadcasting.

Now in her forties, Raphael talks about how she wanted to be an actress but was discouraged from that, so she enrolled in several broadcasting courses at Columbia University. Although she felt ready for the marketplace, she found she couldn't even get a job as a page. Her present success is the result of a long string of failures. She has been fired *eighteen* times. "Sometimes the station changed format. Sometimes it was sold or went dark. One time, the station changed languages on me!" Other times the station management didn't agree with her style.

Sally Raphael has learned to handle failure. She recently commented that the same personality that NBC was paying "big bucks" to broadcast "was turned down by everybody on the face of the earth. But I don't want to sound bitter. I'm not. It was always a wonderful 'adventure' to load up the car and head on." Why did Sally consider her failure an "adventure," when hundreds of other people would never recover from a similar succession of blows?

When I asked David Elias, the successful financial consultant, how he felt when his friends, teachers, and neighbors made fun of him and called him dumb, he replied that he knew he wasn't dumb. He knew he could accomplish whatever he set out to do. He never felt defeated and simply never gave in to the adversity that was heaped upon him. From every indication, Sally Raphael should have given up broadcasting years ago, but by not accepting her losses as failures she could continue to get on with the next "wonderful adventure." It's the way we perceive failure that determines whether it becomes an advantage in the accumulated life's experience or whether it conquers us.

Stop thinking "failure." Strike the word from your vocabulary now. Failure resounds with a finality, like death. Meet adversity with the confidence that important lessons will be learned. Take "failure" out of your writing and speaking. From now on, mistakes, misjudgments, even situations you completely "blow," are temporary interruptions that require some adjustments, nothing more.

◆ Bad Times Need Good Friends

Nearly all of the success-out-of-failure high achievers had someone who believed in them—whether it was a mother or mate, teacher or friend. There was a person who offered unconditional support. It isn't absolutely essential, but it helps. For David Elias, it was his mother who believed in his ability despite teachers who called him "dumb." For Sally Raphael it is her manager, who gave up his own career to manage hers. They now share a life together, and as Sally says, "Somebody had to say each time I was fired, 'Okay, you get twenty-four hours to feel sorry for yourself, then on to the next job.' "

If you really want to progress and grow, to reach those goals, and really live life to its fullest, accept life's catastrophes as a part of your pursuit.

◆◆◆

◆ Make Your Setbacks Work for You

- Always plan to succeed, but when the plan falls through remind yourself that the setback is a valuable opportunity to learn. Remember, whatever happened, it could have been worse!
- Feel the freedom that accompanies a "wipeout." Now it is over, and you know what it feels like. You no longer

have to fear the "dark jaws of failure." It happens to everyone at some time. You have the right to fail, too.

· Strike out the word "failure." Perceive those calamities of life as temporary setbacks, merely inconvenient interruptions on the road to success.

· Accept the responsibility for your part of the failure. Learn to say, "I blew it, it was my fault."

· Don't pass the blame to others when it is your failure.

· Don't blame failure on bad luck or "that's the way the ball bounces."

· Take time to regain your composure and positive attitude. Let bruised pride heal. Get your bearings and regroup.

· Analyze. Take a critical look at your failure. Be the executive producer of your failure, and hold a postproduction meeting.

· Visualize your best, not your worst. Learn from failure. Make adjustments and corrections and then put it out of your mind. Wipe out the mental picture of failure.

· No matter how terrible the failure, you are secure as a human being with talents, abilities, and unique experiences that can be reapplied. You are separate from the failure, and you will be better and stronger than before.

· Look to caring friends and family during times of setbacks and discouragement. They can do wonders for soothing wounds and restoring perspective.

◆◆◆

You *can* bounce back from setbacks. Better yet, bounce ahead!

9

◆

The Lean Machine

---

*I mean to lead a simple
life, to choose a simple shell I can carry
easily—like the hermit crab.*

—ANNE MORROW LINDBERGH, Gift from the Sea

◆ *Operate Lean!*

So much of life is spent accumulating things, then managing them, then exchanging, remodeling, trading, recovering, repairing. In *The Essays of E. B. White,* White wisely suggested, "The home is like a reservoir equipped with a check valve: The value permits influx, but prevents outflow."

This may be the "disposable society," but more comes in than gets thrown out. Half the time we aren't aware of the rapid rate at which we acquire things, and those very things that we thought were needed to enhance our existence can, over time, build up around us and choke off true growth like weeds strangling the blossoms of spring. Upon the heap of things add people, institutions, schedules, spouse, children, pets, special occasions, hobbies, and you have an organizational nightmare! Such a complex system could reduce a management genius to hysteria.

Like most of the women I knew in my "subdivision" years, I was totally consumed by the creation of the "monster machine" that our family had created. My former husband and I worked so hard to acquire a home, two kids, two cars, two pets, and an active social life, all requiring tremendous time and attention. One or the other constantly needed shots, an oil change, an exterminator, snow tires, a baby-sitter, a party, or a plunger. As soon as we got rid of the gophers that were tearing up the lawn, the dogs had to be wormed. It seemed that I barely got the Christmas trays put away and it was time to have a dinner party. One time I had to have a wisdom tooth removed surgically, and it developed into a painful dry socket, putting me out of commission as the systems manager. Talk about breakdowns!

The boys had been bringing me little trays of Kool-Aid and potato chips, but after three days of that diet I hobbled into the kitchen. The only things I could find to eat were hardened brown sugar, bouillon cubes, and soy sauce. The firewood had been dumped in the middle of the driveway instead of being stacked out back. No one had clean socks, jeans, or underwear, and the dogs had devoured the last of the hot-dogs and doughnuts. The plants were turning yellow, the bills hadn't been paid, and there was no cash since I hadn't been to the bank. My absence had caused irreparable confusion to the nursery school carpool. Bill's shirts were still at the laundry, so he was now down to the red cowboy number with pearl buttons; he assured me that it *would* show under the gray pinstripe suit and burgundy tie. It was so bad that the thought of getting well made me sick! It would take weeks to hack my way through the mess.

That was my first look into the voracious mouth of the monster that was gradually making me a slave. As I began to think about the part-time work possibilities outside the home, it became apparent that an attempt to seek my own identity would be doomed unless I trained the organizational monster to heel! What was even more disconcerting was that I continued to believe that a smooth-running, well-organized life was impossible for me. It's true that I saw other families that seemed to have their act together. I also read astonishing reports about women who had returned to their jobs as corporate executives a week after giving birth, with time left over to raise thoroughbreds, design clothes, paint landscapes, and attend gourmet cooking classes. But I attributed those stories to family money, live-in relatives, or just sensational journalism. For a long time the disorganization became an excuse for not setting my own goals. I'm not blaming my husband or family. I'm the one who allowed myself to get drawn into a role that was consuming me and stunting my growth. How could I expect my husband and small children to know what my needs were? Even if I could, would they insist that I get out there and go for it? They had a pretty comfortable life, so why would they volunteer to upset Shangri-la so Mommy could assert herself in the marketplace? It wasn't until I set down some goals for myself that I realized to reach them I would have to do a major reorganization of our family life. I found out that it could be done.

If simple organization is the goal—clean closets and orderly schedules—don't look for lasting effective results, because then what? Is the goal just to sit around, watch the neat piles of towels, and listen to the clock tick? It won't work. If order is the goal, there is a manic-compulsive lurking under those neatly arranged rows of handkerchiefs. Perfect order can become its own monster, enslaving you in the same way as chaos; it can be another excuse to deny yourself the possibility of achievement. A true commitment to an organized life must be part of a broader plan or it does not "take." Just like the dieter who continually loses a few pounds, then immediately gains them back, the "organizer" will go on a binge of straightening, cataloging, reordering, and listing priorities and tasks, then will allow the clutter and disorganization to creep back in and take over.

What we are really talking about is an approach to managing goods, time, and maintenance. Let's first examine goods.

◆ Clean Out the Clutter

I've often wondered if there is a Packrats Anonymous. Collecting, accumulating, and storing things can be a real addiction. Now I'm as big a "nester" as anyone. I love to be surrounded with the things that make me feel secure, that remind me of the past, or that represent something special. I used to save my prom corsages and all the bouquets I received as Miss Nebraska. I had packing boxes of crumbling brown roses and carnations, tied with crushed, mildewed ribbons. It wasn't easy to toss them out. I had to ask myself how long I would need the dried-up reminders of teenage romance or my crowned appearance at a county fair to feel important or special. I ask that question each time I have difficulty discarding something I no longer use or that no longer means anything to my present life: How much longer do I need this?

When I met Roger, who later became my husband, he was in transition from his role as a college professor and administrator to that of an independent television consultant. Over the years he had accumulated a personal library that would have been the envy of any municipal library in Nebraska! In addition, he had saved a roomful of files on nearly everything remotely linked to communications. He also had files on all of his graduate students and collections of notes from all the classes he had ever taught. He packed and paid to move fifteen thousand pounds of household goods to Princeton, and that was *after* he had sorted it!

One day I drove up to his house in Princeton to find a mountain of garbage bags piled at the end of the driveway. Like a demon he was dumping file after file, reams of paper into bags. Boxes of books were stacked for the used-book sale, and cartons of doctoral-dissertation drafts and research materials fluttered to their doom. The garage had been so jammed with boxes and filing cabinets that it functioned as a warehouse, leaving the car to weather the storms in the driveway. Roger looked up with a crazed gleam in his eye. When I asked what was going on, he said, "This feels wonderful. It's like peeling off scales of the past. All this stuff has been holding me back . . . and it's been damn hard on the car!"

The fact is that we really don't need much to live comfortably. I knew that if I was going to achieve my goals, I had to simplify my life so I would be free to direct my time and energy toward getting what I wanted. Like Roger, my first phase of simplifying was to strip down to the bare essentials. I was amazed at how few things I actually needed and how smoothly I could operate without the rest. It was quite a liberating feeling. That's when I learned the joy of operating lean.

◆ Organization Specialists

For those who can afford it, there are "closetologists" who specialize in designing superclosets. Their standard approach is to organize clothes according to occasion, length, season, and color, with separate spaces for shoes, handbags, hats, and furs (when they aren't in storage or the vault).

Dani Needham, wife of film director Hal Needham, manages her wardrobe expertly. She lists every item in her closet by number in a small book she always carries with her. Wherever she may be traveling she always has a complete wardrobe inventory. "If I'm in Paris and I find a purple suit that I want to buy, then I need a lavender blouse. So I look in my book to see if I have one." By numbering each item she can have her housekeeper send "number 52" without any confusion or mistakes.

Closets seem to be getting more attention than kitchens these days. I did a videotaped segment with a New York designer who had managed to computerize a closet for a broadcasting executive. His clothes were arranged according to season and activity on a mechanized conveyor rack. Each clothing category was programmed into a computer in the wall by the closet door. When his client punched in the code for "winter-business," the rack automatically brought around that section and stopped in front of the opened door for his selection.

For help with general organization there are a number of agencies in major cities that are doing very well cleaning up after the packrats of the world. I talked to the founder of Let-Millie-Do-It, a New York–based service that gets into the closets of nearly every brand of the species. According to Millie, the two categories that collect the fastest, or the longest (depending on whether you think in terms of time or space), are clothes and papers. She says much of her time is spent just trying to figure out how her clients can get more into smaller Manhattan spaces. She's devised ways to crowd more under beds, concealed on turntables, and on top of tall cabinets and armoires. She frequently works on ten-foot ladders, because the high ceilings of old New York apartments force her to stack up instead of under. When I asked what her clients' most common request was, she exclaimed, "More closets!" Millie finds that most people have difficulty disposing of anything. Instead they will pay for someone to find a way to keep everything. When Millie strongly recommends discarding, she does it only with the client's approval. Even so Millie finds that some clients actually retrieve the castoffs from the garbage. That conjures up the sad image of someone paying for a service that is so emotionally wrenching that in the darkness they drag the pitiful refuse back into their life to pad the nest with emotional insulation and security.

Stephanie Winston, author of *The Organized Executive,* will straighten up your life for a fee of five hundred dollars a day. She will do everything from organize kitchen cabinets, closets, and books to working out a chore plan for the children. However, I cannot imagine how a stranger, albeit an expert, can know how you want your closets arranged, where you want to keep the electric mixer, or what to keep or discard. Organizing is a highly personal activity, and the process alone is important in developing a more systematic approach to life. I would not presume to know my own mother's preference in organization, and certainly not that of a complete stranger. Also, there is the troubling idea that once again we must turn to an outside source, and an expensive one at that, to take charge of our mess and get us straightened out. There are many jobs that can and should be carried out by hired help, but when it comes to organizing, I prefer to push up my sleeves, dig in, and throw out. It becomes a physical expression of closing out another chapter and moving on to the next. It's good therapy that leaves me refreshed and pleased with my work. There is nothing like "starting fresh" with a clean closet or garage each spring and fall.

◆ Dig In and Throw Out

Rainy weekends are perfect for getting organized, but don't wait for gloomy weather to unload the accumulated weight of your "special collections." If the first glance at your pile of life's residuals leaves you overwhelmed, plan a methodical approach to attack the task over a period of time. Try listing each area that needs attention, then block out days on the calendar for garage, attic, cabinets, basement, and so on. That way you can see it coming and you can get "psyched up" for it. To avoid the dread that usually precedes this unpopular task, start planning so you actually look forward to it.

◆ The Advance Attack

1. Block out clean-up days on the calendar well in advance, and keep this appointment you've made with yourself.

2. Buy a supply of large, sturdy garbage bags, set aside a pair of old work gloves, and collect boxes for the larger items.

3. Plan some special "treat breaks" with unusual drinks and snacks—something you rarely buy, like smoked oysters, caviar, or an exotic fruit and cheese tray.

4. Plan a special reward for yourself at the end of the day—a luxurious bubble bath or muscle soak, or perhaps an elegant dinner or evening at the theater.

5. If you plan to move heavy equipment or furniture, call Hire-a-Kid or someone to help.

◆ The AntiClutter Campaign

1. Start early. Set the alarm for 6:30 or 7:00 A.M.

2. Select your work "look" carefully. If it's dirty work, protect your hands with work gloves, wear a hat or a scarf. Make sure you wear comfortable clothes that are old but not unsightly. Wear makeup and earrings if it makes you feel better.

3. Make the working space as pleasant as possible. If the lighting is bad, bring in an extra lamp. Set up a portable radio or cassette player.

4. Stay with the project until it is finished. If it's a two-day job, plan a time and place to stop. For example, "I will work until 5:30; by that time I plan to have the work area in the garage sorted, including the paint and tools. Tomorrow I will clean the storage boxes."

◆ *Criteria for Disposal*

Cleaning out the clutter is tedious and messy, but for most of us the hardest part is deciding what to keep and what to throw away.

1. Create four piles: Throw Away, Give Away, Fix It, and Maybe.

2. Ask yourself, "Have I used this in the past year?" "Yes" means keep it; "No" is Throw Away.

3. Ask yourself, "Have I worn this in the past year?" "Yes" means keep it; "No" is Throw Away. (That's not too difficult, is it?)

4. "Can I imagine ever needing this?" If "Yes," would it make more sense to buy a new one?

5. "Would I use this if it worked?" Put it in the Fix It pile if "Yes," the Throw Away pile if "No."

6. "Does it have an important meaning to me?" (Awards, trophies, photos.) If "Yes," how much? If it's a keep or a Maybe, check your decision in six months.

The Throw Away pile goes in garbage bags for the garbage collector. The Give Away pile should be packed in boxes to be sent to someone you know who likes hand-me-downs or to charitable organizations like Goodwill or the Salvation Army. Go through the Fix It pile and decide if each article you've saved is worth the time and money to fix it. If so, put it in the car and arrange for the repairs as soon as possible. Do it right away! Go through your Maybe pile to see if there are articles that sneaked through your first cut. I've found that a second close look eliminates half the Maybe pile.

Be tough . . . stay with it, and don't stop until you have a lean machine. It can be a joy to walk into the closet, or go to the garage for a hammer, or open a drawer and know exactly where the blue thread is stored. Remember, organization becomes a way of living, so plan on service checks every few months. I learned to save less, so the anticlutter marches are now conducted on a much smaller scale. Don't wait until spring or fall to give away books, items of clothing, or some of your useless accumulations, if you already know you will never use them.

Print signs on four boxes in your garage or basement: Throw Away, Give Away, Fix It, and Maybe. Then, as things accumulate, toss them into the appropriate box. Get the entire family into the habit of thinking and living with organization as a continual process. Before long the biannual cleaning days will be minor projects instead of awesome, exhausting jobs. The whole family will enjoy a smoother operation without being encumbered by clutter.

Beware of getting so hooked on organization that it becomes an end in itself. Remember, an organized life frees you to pursue your real goals and to fully enjoy life.

◆ How Much Time Do You Have?

There never seems to be enough time. Think how many times you hear "I just ran out of time," or "There just aren't enough hours in the day." Time is our most valuable possession, but do we protect it as we do our other valuables? Have you ever heard of anyone installing a burglar alarm to protect their time? You would be shocked at the idea of throwing twenty-dollar bills into the garbage disposal, but how often do you think nothing of frittering away hours on wasteful activities? Just as we tend to overload the closets with superfluous junk, we can stuff our precious days and night with useless drivel. Achieving goals, reaching for a high purpose, demands extra time, and nothing is going to change or grow without spending the time to get what we want.

It's true that maintaining the status quo is a full-time job—more than a full-time job. I heaped myself with ways to fill my time. I was busy, but not fulfilled. Too often we confuse being active with being productive or satisfied. That was another way I could avoid the real issue, my angry frustration. I didn't enjoy making beds, peeling potatoes, or scraping off the baked-on grease. I would spend hours on the telephone with friends talking about mindless trivia—clothes, menus, children. I bought a wig and spent days trying to wrestle it into some shape that would look "natural" on me. I knitted, painted, polished, and refinished. I collected weeds and made dried-flower arrangements. I made candles, fringed placemats, hemmed napkins. I rearranged and decorated until I realized that I was thirty-six years old. Was I going to spend the rest of my life making things look pretty?

◆ *Time to Save*

Time, our most valuable possession, cannot be replaced, and it cannot be insured. Watch over your time as carefully as you do your money. Think of a "time checking account." Each day there is an automatic deposit of twenty-four hours to your account, and you begin to write checks on it immediately. You must spend it all; this bank will not carry over savings. You are not allowed to write ten-hour checks for "work." You must have receipts for each activity comprising work. Will you spend one hour commuting? One hour cooking? Four hours in business meetings? Two hours for lunch? Four hours watching television? How is each of the twenty-four hours spent? Are you a wise and prudent investor? At the end of the day reconcile your time checking account. It should balance or you are either losing time or getting robbed. What do you have to show for your hours spent?

During the 1982 railroad strike in New York, Roger and I found that because of the tremendous increase in traffic we were spending an hour and a half each way instead of the usual hour. We did a rough calculation and were shocked to find that our daily three-hour commute represented seven hundred and fifty hours a year, or a full month of our lives! Since commuting is one of our least favorite pastimes, we have made adjustments that have reduced the total number of days we spend in the city each week, and we avoid rush hours. On my on-air days I've cut the commuting in half; not too many people are on the road at 5:30 A.M.

When Roger walked into my life back at WCPO-TV in Cincinnati he was carrying a pocket calendar. I had never set eyes on him before, but it was my job to set up an interview with him for an *In Person* segment on children's programming. I watched in amazement as he turned page after page of days filled with appointments, lists, and names. Incredulous, I joked that it looked as if we would have to plan to video-

tape in early 1993. Later I found that he also had four phone
lines and an answering service, so when he wasn't keeping an
appointment he was answering the telephone or returning
messages. He could have as many as thirty-five to fifty messages a day. While I had been rearranging and decorating,
Roger had been scheduling and phoning. Both of us had done
a terrific job at being busy, but how far had all that activity
really moved us ahead?

When you begin to subtract those hours of empty business, like money drawn from the time checking account, you
become price-conscious. It would never occur to me to buy an
expensive appliance or outfit without first asking the price.
Yet most of the time we plunge into a new project or plan an
activity without any notion of what the final cost will be in
our time. Estimate the cost before you spend, and don't forget,
those nickels and dimes in time add up!

When I decided on my goal of finding a professional role
in television, I knew that to achieve it would require some
tricky changes in our living pattern; namely, I had to organize
my time differently. It came together over years of trial and
error, interviewing working couples and single mothers, and
reading all the latest books on home and office management.
Like cleaning closets, managing time is a very personal en-
deavor. While much can be learned from experts, some elements must be worked out according to highly individual
preferences. How can someone else's rule of limiting phone
calls to fifteen minutes apply to me, when my work requires
long phone conversations researching and preinterviewing a
guest for an appearance on *Today?* If I have not talked to my
mother in two or three weeks, I certainly want to talk longer
than fifteen minutes. However, my phone calls generally have
a purpose. There is little idle chitchat just because I am bored.
It is simply too costly—in time.

Let me share some of the time management techniques
that have been incorporated into our overall system. I say
"our" because our whole family is involved. The system really
works for us. Many of these suggestions will work for you,
too, but better yet, some will provide the inspiration for your
own system. True organization is adaptive. It should bend

and change with your needs, create a climate for achievement and growth.

◆ Invest in Your Time

Each year we buy new calendars. Roger and I each keep a large office calendar. We maintain another large family calendar with large blank spaces for each day by the kitchen phone, which is also the family message center. My son Bill has his own large blotter calendar on his desk, and Roger and I keep individual pocket calendars with two pages for each day. That sounds cumbersome, but it is the best way for three very busy people to coordinate our daily schedules. All regularly scheduled activities are filled in on all the calendars: Bill's drum lessons on Wednesday, meetings, classes, and the like. All medical appointments are faithfully recorded, dinners with friends, theater and concerts, dog grooming, school track meets and band concerts, overnight guests, vacations, business travel—everything. Roger and I make special note of any business travel on the family calendar. We have to be careful that our travel plans do not collide. If one of us is away, the other stays at home. In that way, the operation runs smoothly without complication or difficulty, while providing essential continuity for our family.

Bill has the responsibility of keeping a record on his calendar of school activities, report-card and term-paper dates, exams, social functions, and concerts and coordinating his records with the family calendar. The pocket calendars that Roger and I carry are the mobile combination of both business and family schedules. No matter where we are we have the entire month's calendar in purse or briefcase. Tucked into our pocket calendars we each have a personal phone directory, so that no matter where we are we have important phone numbers at our fingertips—family doctor, pharmacy, school office, family members, and important business associates. Writing something down frees you from having to remember it and allows your mind to work on more important matters. It takes a few extra seconds to record information and transfer it to another calendar, but you are then liberated from having to recall detailed and often forgettable information.

Batik artist Sara Eyestone, the remarkable lady to whom I have often referred, keeps a five-year calendar. In addition to writing down all the activities for herself, her husband, and her four children, the family uses the calendar as a goal-setting device. The results have been phenomenal. Sara's younger daughter, Amy, wants to spend a semester studying in France and has had it on the calendar for three years. Her older sister's objective to attend school in Switzerland became a reality through the same long-range planning.

◆ *Get Listed*

By now the whole world should know the value of list making. Everyone I know makes lists! We recently packed Bill off to summer camp, and during the preparation I was delighted to find in his scrawl a precamp list on the refrigerator/message center: batteries, shampoo, insect repellent, junk food. It was his reminder to himself. In previous years, I was the master camp list maker and "divine reminder," a role I am happy to pass on.

We make a trip to the food market every two weeks, so the grocery list is very important. When we run low on milk or eggs one of us stops at the neighborhood convenience store. But under no circumstances will we spend more than three hours a month loading and unloading a grocery cart. To make that work we have to religiously list everything we run out of, plan two weeks of meals, and make certain that we buy enough to last two weeks. With the help of a big freezer, many people manage to avoid the supermarket for up to a month!

After grocery shopping we list the food on hand and the meals for each evening dinner. The meals are simpler now, no baked Alaska or homemade stuffed cabbage rolls. Monday through Friday the time limit for meal preparation is one hour a day. If it takes more than an hour, it goes into the crockpot. I have become an expert in "slow cooking."

We keep a separate list for clothes, household items, and gifts, and by anticipating the monthly needs, everything can be accomplished in one trip. We never make a trip for a single item.

I also keep a list of daily chores in my pocket calendar. On top I list business calls and jobs to be done. The bottom half is devoted to personal reminders—calls, repairs, errands. When our family schedule becomes especially hectic or demanding, the list system is in place, and although the load is heavier, checking off each item brings the satisfaction of an obligation well met.

Mel and Sheryl London are an extraordinary couple. Together they own and operate a film company, Symbiosis, Inc. Their filmmaking has taken them all over the world; their clients include a major international airline and many Fortune 500 companies. They have written twelve books—some together, some individually. Mel, best known as the author of *Bread Winners,* was nominated for an Academy Award for one of his documentary films. Sheryl is a talented painter and has a waiting list of people who want to buy her work. They live in a sizable Manhattan apartment and maintain a second home on Fire Island, an hour's drive to the ferry and a twenty-minute ride to their house. There are no supermarkets, hardware stores, or cars on Fire Island, so everything has to be hauled in by bag or cart. I couldn't believe they were so composed and had time for their writing, to say nothing of their leisurely bike rides around the island and long walks up the beach. Completely baffled, I asked them how in the world they managed such a complex system with no help.

"It all begins with color coding," explained Sheryl. "We work with four categories: pink cards for books to read; green for hardware and clothing needs; white for groceries and supplies for the New York apartment; and yellow for groceries for Fire Island. We keep these working lists posted on the wall by the phone, and at a glance I can see what goes where." In addition to their color codes, they both keep a pocket calendar/date book with their combined projects and commitments along with their individual schedules. It's truly amazing to see how much Mel and Sheryl are able to accomplish and produce as a result of their unique system of organization.

◆ *File Away Instead of While Away*
When I became a single parent it quickly became ap-

parent that I would have to manage everything from car and household insurance to rental contracts, routine maintenance, and a hundred daily responsibilities. To help me get organized, I bought a sturdy, bright yellow standard-sized file cabinet. It's one of the best investments I've ever made. In fact, it still serves me well. Almost everything in my life has a file folder: cars, banks, bills, schools, clubs, contracts, receipts, income-tax records. I assign a file folder to each son for grades, letters, awards, anything too good for the bulletin board. Now I don't worry about where to find important papers. Each year I clean out and update. Generally families are run from a couple of shoeboxes or small metal lockboxes. But why not approach the operation of a family as you would a business? Installing a comprehensive family filing system in a commercial-type file cabinet is a good way to keep the lean machine running smoothly.

◆ *Night Work*

I thought that I was fairly organized before we moved to New York and I joined *Today*. However, when the days started at 4:30 or 5:00 A.M., a few problems turned up in my neat little system which forced me to make further refinements that proved to be super time-savers.

My day really begins the night before. During the two years I co-hosted *A.M. Buffalo* I never had to worry about my clothes. A local department store loaned me a different on-air outfit every day. Since *Today* does not have a similar arrangement, I was faced with the considerable cost of building a wardrobe and the daily decision of what to wear. On the days I appear on the air, I leave the house before Roger and Bill are up, so to make the home life as normal as possible I got in the habit of hanging out everything I intend to wear the night before. I mean everything: panty hose, jewelry, belt, the works. I make sure my script and any business materials are packed in my briefcase. I look over the list of things to do the next day to make certain I have my files, books, or research materials. Then either Roger or I set the table for breakfast and make a note of reminders for Bill. Over the past four years Bill has assumed many of these "prelaunch" habits, so he does his own night-before planning. Now, even on days I do not have to leave early, I find that the night-before routine gives me a head start on the day. It's another way to free my mind from the trivia that can be so nettlesome.

◆ *Pack It Up*
Almost a month before vacation we routinely pull the travel folder from the file cabinet. We post the "things we wish we had" list on the refrigerator. These are the items we never thought to bring on the last trip. It provides a working list for vacation travel. I also have a list of favorite travel outfits. By consulting it before packing, I save a lot of time usually spent deciding what to wear.

Both Roger and I have jobs that require a certain amount of travel, usually trips of only one to three nights. We found that the night-before preparation was taking too much time—selecting clothes, bagging up toilet articles, papers, and accessories. We have reduced our travel preparation time to about ten minutes by having prepacked bags. We both have nylon plastic kits that contain:

> travel-size shampoo
> powder
> soap
> shower cap
> razor
> sewing kit
> hair spray
> toothpaste
> travel alarm
> cleansing cream
> travel dryer
> wine corkscrew
> travel clock
> perfume

In a separate bag we have a small plastic collection of bottles containing drug items: aspirin, decongestant, Band-Aids, vitamins, nasal spray, prescription medicines, eye drops, sinus medication.

The medication bag has been a lifesaver on countless occasions. In fact, I now carry it with me in my handbag.

Before I began life as a working professional, I would throw a tube of lipstick or blusher into my handbag. Now it is important that I have a complete miniature makeup kit for touch-ups in my handbag at all times. The extra time, money, and planning it took to accumulate these bags have paid off. It is especially liberating to go to the closet and know my travel bag is packed and ready to go. What a relief it is to know that my nasal spray is with me when the sniffles hit, that I have aspirin for the headaches after a long session in the editing room. Consequently, I get very few headaches because I can be more relaxed and confident knowing that the calendars, lists, and file folders are keeping the family/professional systems in place. I don't have to remember everything. The information or the article is there when I need it, and I can get on with more important work.

◆ Maintenance: The Unmentionable

Maintenance is one of those facts of life. Everything we own requires a certain amount of maintenance—home, yard, cars, pet, boats. Property is an investment, and if it is to hold its value, you have to face the fact that it is going to require time and attention. Before considering any new acquisition, it is wise to consider the maintenance costs in your time as well as money.

My life as a homemaker was definitely a high-maintenance life—lots of rebuilding, refinishing, repairing. I got a kick out of it then, but now who has the time for all that redoing and upkeep? I get much more excitement from personal accomplishment. It is impossible to move ahead toward achieving any new objectives if you are buried under the never-ending demands of routine maintenance. The maintenance monster will devour you! Something always needs to be serviced, cleaned, repaired, replaced, dropped off, picked up, moved, mowed, raked, repotted, replanted, and reseeded. We're talking about the furnace filters of life, and they come in a hundred different sizes . . . no one ever sees them. No one cares if you spent half a day jeopardizing your health in a crawl space looking for the filter clamps. Have you ever heard anyone boast, "I changed the furnace filters today. Can you smell the cleaner air?"

Today our family is committed to a low-maintenance life-style. Here is how to tame the maintenance monster: Get help. We decided what we enjoyed doing ourselves, like planting fall and spring flowers, caring for the roses and shrubs, and watching the birch and lilac mature. We don't do windows! We both spent enough time in our separate battles with the grub worms and gophers, so now we pay $172 a year for a lawn service. We still do the mowing and raking, and Bill pitches in to help. He also takes care of the garbage, manages the firewood, unloads the dishwasher, and handles a variety of tasks.

Build a task force to help with the maintenance monster. Plug into the seasonal rhythm of your maintenance needs. Do you need a carpet-cleaning service? Seasonal window cleaning? Snow removal? Lawn care? When are your cars due for routine service? Do you need furnace and air-conditioning checks? Get estimates. Read ads. Try out local services. Try calling a high school placement service. Be innovative. Place an ad, look for retirees, post a sign on the "help wanted" bulletin boards in the post office and grocery store. Contact the president of your church's youth group. Develop your own task force of maintenance assistants. Include them in your family filing system. Watch them turn up on your yearly calendar. It is another way to buy time. You may think you can't afford some of these services, but how much do you value your time? How many years of your life can you afford? Remember, we all have time deposits of only twenty-four hours a day. How will you spend yours?

Here are some tips on how to build your own "lean machine":

◆◆

- Clean out the clutter! Get rid of everything that isn't absolutely necessary. The journey to success is easier if you travel light.
- Be a time miser. Do a "time audit" and find out if you are wasting time or if others are robbing you. Keep a daily account of how you spend each minute of your twenty-four hours.
- Manage your time more efficiently:
    a. Keep calendars at home, in the office, and in your handbag or briefcase.
    b. Make lists: food menus, chores, business objectives, phone calls, errands.
    c. Develop a filing system for every element of your life.
- Begin the day the night before. Hang out clothes and accessories for the next day. Pack briefcase and purse, make lists. Check the menu to see if food needs special preparation. Leave messages for family and service helpers.
- Be ready to go. Have your bags packed with toilet articles, medications, makeup. The medication bag and makeup kit are great to keep in purse or briefcase for daily use.
- Get help with the maintenance monster. Build a task force of regular service agencies and personnel to help handle the jobs that hold you back. Be innovative in finding helpers.

◆◆

Enjoy the freedom of operating a lean machine. Feel the extra-soft breezes of extra time and energy that come from having an organized life—a system that liberates rather than enslaves.

Make the investment in time to develop an organizational style that pays dividends for life!

10

◆

Harness Emotions

*A man who is
swayed by passions may have good enough
intentions, may be truthful in word,
but he will never find the truth.*

—GANDHI

*The principal use of prudence,
of self-control, is that it teaches us
to be masters of our passions. . . .*

—DESCARTES

◆ *Anger*

MY SON JEFF, now nineteen, was a precocious toddler, super-active, and verbal. He had a short attention span with the energy level of a wild rhino. We did everything: fingerpainted all over the kitchen, made Play-Doh from scratch, built kites, entertained other three-year-olds, collected caterpillars, and prayed that nursery school would expand to an all-day program. During one of the "well-baby" checks at the pediatrician's, the doctor congratulated me on Jeff's good health and development. I stood before him, hollow-eyed, haggard, feeling absolutely beaten, occasionally scratching my hives. I had the overwhelming impulse to attack him, to go for his throat, stomp on his stethoscope, rip out his thinning hair, and dig my penny-loafer into his sagging groin. I was shocked at the intensity of my emotions. I had no idea that my emotional "buffer zone" had worn so thin that a well-meaning remark from the pediatrician would make me see red. I didn't even know *why* I had "ignited." Hot tears boiled up in my eyes and sizzled down my cheeks. Like many women, I had learned to control the tears of sadness, but the tears of anger and frustration were baffling, always breaking forth at the most inconvenient, embarrassing times. Driving home in the privacy of the Pinto station wagon, I broke down; the tears erupted like hot lava, and I really didn't know what was wrong. I was mad as hell and I didn't even know it. In trying to be the ideal mother, I had denied my frustrations and repressed my anger. I had neglected my own needs to learn, to grow, and to socialize. The tears and temper flare-ups were safety-valve releases, signaling the need to make some adjustments. That's easy for me to say now. Meanwhile, mothers all over America continue to squelch the urge to lunge at their pediatricians, explode at salesclerks, and scream at husbands and lovers. Anger, frustration, and jealousy produce negative reactions that erode our relationships and interfere with personal achievement and growth. Until we understand our emotional rivers, learn to read their currents and control their destructive powers, our achievements will be seriously impeded in our drive to our goals.

Now I don't presume to be an authority on emotions. Indeed, it has been difficult to find scientific research on the subject. Charles Darwin was the first to take an interest in human emotions. By the early part of this century he had brought some of the best minds to the subject for closer examination. But emotions as a focus for study soon fell out of favor because of its "subjective nature." Behavior, which could be more easily measured, became the darling of modern psychological research. Recently, however, there has been a glimmer of interest in the study of human emotions. The latest research involves analyzing facial muscles and monitoring "brain activity and autonomic arousal." (Yawn.)

In the meantime, we struggle with the bewildering power of our own emotions. And no wonder! On one end of the emotional spectrum, anger can cloud rational thought, drain us of energy, rob our creativity, alienate us from others—even from ourselves—and bury our goals. At the other end, love can bring us ecstasy and joy, make us compassionate and sharing, restore a sense of well-being and belonging. Love can give us hope, tolerance, and generosity. It can fuel our dreams and aspirations, stimulate achievement, and fly us toward our goals.

But who is in control? Are you the one steadily guiding your emotional boat through turbulent currents, or are you tossed about helplessly as a passenger of your own emotions?

We get little training in managing emotion; it's another one of those important skills that we have to pick up along the way. When we were little, Mom or Dad stepped in and told us how to behave or simply took over the situation—took responsibility. As adolescents our first emotional encounters took us by storm. We may grow more independent during those years, and we may begin to learn to manage time, but instruction in managing emotion is left to trial and error, highs and lows, euphoria and heartbreak. I remember how I thought my life would be wrecked if I didn't get asked to the prom by a certain boy. As we mature, we build a history of emotional experiences; we generally learn how to throttle our romantic rushes and cap the anger, but that doesn't necessarily mean that we understand the process and are able not only to manage the feelings, but to actually use them to our advantage.

You can't get rid of emotions. They make us uniquely human. How drab life would be without the glorious spectrum of emotions! High achievers stay tuned to their emotional frequency and are not thrown off-balance by bouts of anger or a whirlwind love affair. Those that make it to their goals learn to enjoy their rich emotional colors without being blinded by them, and often the energy generated by emotion can actually be channeled into constructive purposes that enhance goal striving and completion.

◆ Be Angry—Don't Be Angry

Anger tends to be misunderstood, is confusing or frightening. I was told not to be angry or that it wasn't "ladylike." "If you're going to be angry, leave the room." "Apologize for being angry." Thus many of us form the habit of denying anger or stifling it, then suffering the consequences later. Society presents grossly conflicting signals concerning the management of anger. On the one hand, we are told that a display of anger is unbecoming, shows a lack of control, "bad breeding." On the other hand, we are told not to repress anger, to "let it out" in socially acceptable ways. Psychiatrist David Viscott states, "Unexpressed anger can poison relationships, rob us of happy times, and insidiously destroy the joy in life." According to psychiatrist Gerald Kushel, anger should not be denied or repressed. It can cause psychosomatic heart disease, ulcers, migraine headaches, and backaches. Repressed anger has also been known to be the cause of sexual difficulties, to say nothing of the havoc it can cause a relationship.

◆ *What Is Anger?*

You want to see an instant angry reaction? Ask anyone to tell you about the times they waited all day for a furniture deliveryman or a telephone installer who didn't show up. Or about trying to get a mistake corrected on their electric bill. Whenever we feel deceived or helpless, whenever we are not shown the respect or cooperation or service or treatment we deserve, we feel angry.

During my frustrated-homemaker period, I often experienced the kind of anger caused by the "riffraff" treatment. I signed up with a local modeling agency in an effort to keep up with the outside world and pick up some extra "pin" money. The "look-see" interviews were really demeaning. There I was with thirty or forty girls (some in their teens), waiting for hours while somebody took his own sweet time getting around to checking me out to see if I were "worthy" of going through the same process again with fewer applicants and then, if I were lucky, again with only three or four. Now I had to schedule carefully, I was paying a baby-sitter, there were meals to worry about and errands to run . . . the indignity of it all! Waiting for hours brought me to a slow burn. I could feel the anger begin to tingle in my toes and slowly boil up to my carefully blushed cheeks. After all, I was the mother of two, I had a successful husband, a nice home, I gave lovely parties, and besides . . . I had Rosenthal china! For some odd reason the Rosenthal china stuck in my mind, and through the years, whenever I found myself in situations where I was treated with less respect than I preferred, I tacitly reminded myself that I had Rosenthal china. "Surely those people must not realize that I own Rosenthal china!" It was like a secret little code to myself—a reminder that I was feeling angry. Even today, the Rosenthal china trick helps restore perspective and brings me a smile.

We all want to feel special, somehow different from everyone else, and when we become just another face in the crowd, another number waiting for service, another applicant waiting to be processed, we feel threatened, a mild form of fear. In his book *Centering,* Kushel tells us that fear is the basis of anger. He states that the physical manifestations of anger are the same as fear: increased adrenaline flow, tight stomach, clenched jaw and/or fist, shortness of breath, a general "fight or flight" tension. Do you know how your anger feels? Is it like a hot flash, slow burn, or years of simmer?

◆ Recognize Anger

My vague discontent and frustration during the 1970s grew out of anger, although I didn't recognize it at the time. I was stuck at home while my husband pursued a career, and I was losing out on experiences, travel, friends, and income. My hot tears and baffling hostile feelings toward the pediatrician that day also grew out of anger, but before I could move ahead and make the necessary changes in my life, I had to first recognize that I was angry, then figure out why. When you feel the symptoms of anger, whether they are hot flashes of aggression, the slow burn that begins in the toes, or the internal brew of repressed anger that may fester over years, recognize it. Understand and define those feelings of anger. Then look for the origin. Ask yourself:

- What do I fear?
- Do I fear pain?

- Do I fear loss of something?
- Do I fear rejection or separation?
- Do I fear failure?
- Have I been violated?
- Has there been a violation of my time? My space? My property?
- Have I been deceived or cheated?
- Do I feel helpless? Exposed? Vulnerable?

Add your own questions that will help you identify anger. Then ask yourself why—what's causing it? Give yourself permission to be angry; it's perfectly natural. Being angry isn't bad or abnormal. Accept your anger as you accept your talents and skills. It's an unavoidable part of being a human and living an active life.

◆ Deal with Anger

The spectrum of anger is much like that of color. Anger comes in many different hues and intensities—ranging from gentle pastels to blinding, brilliant reds. Learn your own shades of anger, then take charge of those feelings and blend them into your total personality palette. Don't let anger cloud your vision and keep you from achieving your goals. You can be the master of your anger and even use it to your advantage sometimes.

Martin Luther King, Jr., wrote:

> When I am angry I can write, pray, and preach well, for then my whole temperament is quickened, my understanding sharpened, and all mundane vexations and temptations gone.

Many find that a light touch of anger gives them an edge. The old "I'll show 'em" attitude often gives us the drive to do our best or try our hardest.

Lee Iacocca made this statement famous: "Don't get mad—get even." But such an attitude seethes with rage and revenge, and invites unproductive, destructive reactions. Anger can provide an edge, but don't let it dominate your goals and become an obsession. Stay in charge of anger. How about "Don't get mad—get ahead!" Use the extra energy on your own goals. Don't spend precious time getting even. Focus your resources on what is good for you, on the goals you have set for yourself.

Find ways to tame your anger:

1. GET OUT YOUR "ROSENTHAL CHINA." What is your "Rosenthal china"? When you find yourself in situations that make you mad or frustrated, when you're receiving treatment that is impersonal and demeaning, think of something special you do or have that is yours alone, that sets you apart and reminds you of your life after that moment of anger. Look beyond the present situation and concentrate on your goals. There is a private security in knowing that you have a powerful system of personal achievement and a future that holds what you want.

2. EXPRESS YOUR FEELINGS. Tell the person, "I am very angry with you." "You dented my fender, and I am furious!" "The reports were delivered to the wrong address, and I'm outraged!" By releasing the angry feelings at the time, you dissipate the pressure and reduce potential consequences.

3. WRITE A LETTER! My favorite method of managing anger is to write a letter that is never mailed to the person who has made me angry or to myself, describing in detail the circumstances that have angered me. It works! Describe your emotions in detail. Use colorful, strong language; let it all out on paper. I can't tell you the relief I feel from expressing, without censor, the reasons for my anger, the list of abuses, my intentions of legal action, my demands for retribution. After reading it several times with great satisfaction, I put it aside for a few days before rereading it. Usually my anger is gone, and the letter is torn up. However, in some instances there is a legitimate reason to write a letter and mail it. In those cases, after cooling off, I write a thoroughly professional message devoid of effusive emotion, dealing with facts, not feelings.

4. TAKE A WALK. Physical activity is another effective way

to manage anger. There is nothing quite as releasing as a brisk walk; by brisk I mean intense—really charge, pound the pavement, swing your arms, work at it for a long distance or at least until you are tired.

5. TRY A HOT SOAK! I also recommend a hot bath. I can sink into a hot tub at times when I'm so tense that I can hardly turn my head and twenty minutes later emerge as relaxed as a rag doll. Spas are also good for releasing anger. A good workout, the steam room or sauna, the whirlpool, and even a massage offer great release.

6. SLAM A DOOR! Many families develop rules for dealing with anger. When her four children were growing up, my sister-in-law allowed certain behavior from the children when they were angry. They were not allowed to destroy or damage anything, but she did permit them to slam doors. There have been a few times here at home when something drove me to my wits' end—the kind of anger that makes you want to throw something. I marched down the hall and slammed the door to the bedroom as hard as I could. It felt wonderful. I slammed it again. Three times was all I needed. It provided a satisfying, noisy, and physical release of anger. On those rare occasions, a good door slam is the best remedy for me. Amazingly, the hinges are still secure!

After you've learned to recognize your anger, and define the source, don't be afraid to try out different methods of managing it. Be creative. Select a method appropriate for the setting. In a formal business meeting you can't jump into a hot tub, but you may be able to draw angry cartoons on your notepad, let your imagination focus on your dream house or car, or imagine everyone in the room dressed in drag or shortie pajamas. Some businessmen have dartboards in their offices, or a mini–basketball net. Some play the drums, punch a pillow, or throw a sponge ball. You will find, as have other high achievers, that when you recognize anger and develop effective methods of release and management, it becomes less and less of a problem. You will be free to progress toward your goals without the disruption and delays caused by anger.

◆ *Fear*

Fear is a slippery, unpredictable creature. It can emerge dramatically from our physical and emotional depths to save our life, then reappear as an ugly monster rendering us helpless victims too frightened to move. Fear is also present in feelings of anger and guilt, and it's not always easy to separate fear from the emotional mixture.

Unlike many other emotions, fear originates from the base survival instinct. In his book *Feelings,* Dr. Willard Gaylin explains:

> When we feel fear of a potential impending disaster, the feeling is part of a set of multiple physiological changes that prepare us for either flight from the danger or an attack on it . . . a fight-flight mechanism is an inbuilt part of the emergency response of the organism.

I felt the paralyzing effects of fear as I stood frozen with stage fright before the graduation audience. I also felt the reassuring charge of fear-injected adrenaline as I proved I could make it up the ski lift and back down the slope without falling. The familiar rush of energy and "nerves" just before the camera comes on has become part of the equipment necessary for me to do my best job.

To high achievers, a degree of fear can be beneficial, but at the other end of the scale it can be a monstrous, controlling force that reduces people to cowering, whimpering helplessness. Fear can be a wicked shepherd, confining would-be achievers to a life of strict status quo, avoiding any anxiety, too afraid to take risks, to accept change, to learn anything new, to live a full life! Fear can be the single most limiting influence in life.

One of the reasons so many continue to let fear dominate their decisions and goals is that it has never been identified as fear. We have grown up being told, "Don't be afraid," or, "There's nothing to be afraid of." We might be shrieking with terror. There might be a dog twice our size snarling at us, baring its teeth, but Mommy and Daddy say, "Don't be afraid. The doggie won't bite you." Even a small child understands danger, but we are told not to be afraid. Before a performance we are told not to be nervous, before an operation we are told there is nothing to fear. So through the years we nurture this big fat *lie* to ourselves. Fear is bad, therefore we won't admit that we're afraid or nervous. "Don't be a scaredy-cat." If you're afraid, you're "yellow-bellied," a lowly coward. So we deny fear, redirect it, disguise it, keep it locked away in the closet.

It's Dr. Irene Kassorla's theory that much of the "generalized anxiety" you feel as an adult is a result of fears "planted in your unconscious when you were so small and have their genesis in dangers that you believed existed then. But they were probably only a toddler's distortion of reality."

The toddler's instincts say, "Yes, there *is* something to fear." So he grows up worrying that one of these times the dog will bite, or the performance will be a bust, and that "generalized anxiety" carries over to other behavior. Dr. Kassorla believes that it's the vague, locked-up fears that cause so many cases of alcohol and drug abuse, overeating, over-smoking, and assorted compulsive behaviors, all elaborate devices to avoid the "boogeyman" buried in the unconscious. And he is actually only a shadow, according to Kassorla: "Most of your anxieties will never materialize . . . you can put your childhood ghosts and archaic myths to rest."

◆ Let Fear Out of the Closet

A general consensus among professionals seems to be that the best way to deal with fear is to recognize it as fear, then admit that you feel fearful. Give yourself permission to be afraid, and admit it. Remember, we're all afraid some of the time. It is the coward who can't admit he is frightened; it requires courage to admit to fear.

◆ Honesty Is the Best Medicine

Be honest about your fears, and about how they feel, how much they influence your decisions and the direction of your life. You will be surprised at how they lessen; many just dissolve completely.

As Dr. Irene Kassorla insists, "The way to get out of your fears is to first get into them!" Get them out in the open, talk about them, test them.

When I resolved to conquer the beginner's ski slope, I was afraid of falling, afraid of embarrassment, afraid of failure, afraid of breaking my legs and the pain and inconvenience that accompanies such a catastrophe. I could feel the physical symptoms. My fear inhibited my performance on my first few tries, but as I stubbornly stuck with it, the fear relaxed into more normal cautious behavior.

◆ Don't Let Fear Stop You

When you first want to take a risk, when you want to try something new, don't let fear stop you. New experiences, new opportunities, new people and places can cause some fear. Understand that the unfamiliar will make you feel some of the discomforts of fear—that's normal. But if the new territory brings you closer to your goals, press on, go ahead in spite of your fear. A firm commitment to your goals can usher you through all kinds of perils.

Talk yourself through the fear of new experiences. "I'm feeling frightened and anxious because I've never done this before. This is a strange place with unfamiliar people, equipment, smells, and sounds. After I become more familiar with my role here, I'll be fine. After I've done this a few times, I won't be as uncomfortable. If I can stay with this—keep going—I'll be a step closer to achieving my goal."

When I battled the ski lifts, I told myself that if I could just make it to the top of the slope three times, I'd be satisfied. As it turned out, I became more relaxed, really got involved with the sport instead of my fear, and wanted to continue long after three times. By sticking with my goal of learning to ski, I conquered the fear of the ski lifts and the fear of skiing, and I'm now free of that fear for life!

Don't let fear keep you from leading a full life! Set your sights on your goals, and don't let fear stop you from achieving them.

- Find out what you fear.
- Find out if fear is the cause of any vague anxieties.
- Admit your fear. Don't be afraid to say that you're afraid.
- Talk yourself through new experiences. Remind yourself that it's natural to feel fearful in unfamiliar circumstances.
- Focus on your goals, not your fear. Use your goals for positive energy in managing fear.
- Stay with the new experience! In time you will feel more in control and less frightened, better able to manage the required skills.
- Be comforted by the fact that getting through a fearful experience can free you of that fear for life!
- Knowing how to manage fear can give you new freedom to live a fuller life and to achieve your goals.

◆ Love and Romance

Love is a beautiful, positive emotion. We all strive to love and be loved. We are surrounded with reminders of love, or the illusions of love, in advertisements, movies, television, literature, and theater. For high achievers, love can be a powerful enhancer. But love can also interrupt accomplishments, confuse priorities, and obliterate our goals.

The book *Love and Addiction,* by Stanton Peele and Archie Brodsky, describes ways the "love high can become a crippling influence, lowering self-esteem, sabotaging goals, creating self-defeating behavior, while consuming precious time, sometimes years of our lives."

◆ The Love Junkie

I remember all too well the agonies and ecstasies of early teenage love. The delicious telephone calls—will he call? Will he call Judy instead? There he is—it's him! What to wear, what to say, what to do? Then there were the bitter tears of hurt and disappointment—the wrenching, aching pain. But, ah (swoon), the highs were worth the lows. We all go through it; there is no escape from the lessons of the heart. During that awkward period of development we are fascinated by romance and preoccupied with sex. We collect data, we experiment, and over time we figure out what it's all about and go on. The problem for some people is that they stay on the merry-go-round of love and never learn to get off. "Love makes the world go 'round," and that's just what it does to the "love junkie." They just go around in circles, falling from one romantic "fix" to another, never quite getting on a solid path for goals and achievement. You will hear the love junkie say things like, "One look into those eyes, and I was a goner," or, "One look at that body, and I couldn't think of anything else!" These are the people who like to think there is some force out there that takes over their whole being, and they love it. It provides all kinds of excuses for lack of time, money, direction, and accomplishments. Blame it on love.

H. L. Mencken said, "To be in love is merely to be in a state of perpetual anesthesia." For the love junkie, romantic love can provide an escape from reality.

Without drugs or alcohol, our minds can provide a fantastic escape haven, which in excess can occupy years of time and energy. Such an escape interferes with any commitment to goals or personal achievement, and the blame is always placed on some supernatural "outside" force.

Barbara Cartland, called the "Queen of Romance," has written 378 romantic novels and sold a total of 400 million copies of her books. She understands the anatomy of romantic love. It's her theory that a woman falls in love with her first lover and after that "loves love." Many of her fans write her appreciative letters that tell how wonderful it is that her novels "take me out of myself into a fairyland." To many, her books bring true diversion; others need escape. To others, books alone don't provide enough escape. I had a friend who was in a bad marriage, and rather than deal with her discontent she escaped by drifting from one romantic involvement to another. She insisted that it brought her excitement and diversion. But what was happening to her life? Was her goal to find excitement and diversion? Is maintaining an unhappy marriage a goal? Is finding a new lover a goal? Is cheating on her husband a goal?

◆ *Become the Master of Your Love*

Roger came into my life at the wrong time. I had been separated from my former husband only a few weeks, and Roger's divorce was only seven months old. He was to be a guest on *In Person,* the program I was hosting on WCPO-TV in Cincinnati. I was going through one of the worst periods of my life, and I needed friends and support desperately, but no romance. Roger was director of the media center and professor of communications at the University of Cincinnati, but the reason WCPO-TV suggested that he appear on *In Person* was his involvement in children's television. He had made quite a name for himself as a consultant to the CBS Broadcast Group; since he had also worked with local children's programming, including our station's kids' program, the segment was a natural opportunity to link national and local kids' programs with videotapes of several cute shows. Roger had a wonderfully pedantic air, complete with beard and wire-framed glasses, along with an incongruous sparkle of mischief. I found him to be quite attractive for a professor.

When *In Person* was canceled, and my life began to get darker and more uncertain, Roger offered to help me. He had a number of contacts in the television business and seemed confident of my chances of getting another job in television. I needed help, but no romance. All I could be really sure of was that I could qualify as a short-order cook. Roger suggested that we have dinner, and he offered to help me develop a professional resume. I said, "Wonderful," and I thought, No romance! We developed a decent resume and became frightened friends. Roger gave me a subscription to *Broadcasting* magazine, brought me books on television production and performing. We took the kids to the zoo, charcoaled hamburgers, discussed the future of electronic journalism, saw movies, did errands, and swapped child-care tips, but no romance!

It was only a few months before Roger suggested that we marry. I was mortified . . . no romance! I said, "Don't you know that we're still grieving?" I knew that a deep romantic commitment at that time would be a terrible mistake for us both, yet I needed Roger: he was truly the only bright spot in that very dark period. I also knew that if I were going to make it on my own, if I were going to, at long last, find my own identity, I had to do it myself . . . on my own terms. Romance would have to wait. There were risks to take, failures to overcome, goals to achieve. I'm thankful that Roger respected my need to strike out on my own but stayed close enough to catch me when I fell. As I gained confidence in myself and in my own abilities as a professional and a single mother, romance began to bud . . . but it was very fragile at first and a long way from anything resembling marriage.

It was more than three years before I felt ready for marriage; and it would have to be very different from my first one. Roger and I have built a wonderful working marriage which allows room for individual growth and achievement, yet brings us support, security, trust, sharing, and romance. We have individual goals and shared goals. It's working now because we made earlier decisions about our future. I stayed on track, followed my plan, and we are both benefiting now.

Sound tough, don't I? I am an incurable romantic. I love mushy cards and gifts of fresh flowers. Roger's love poems bring tears to my eyes. When I have to be away from home I hide little love notes around the house for Roger to discover. And when I unpack in my hotel when I travel, I usually find little cards or surprises Roger has tucked in my travel bags. We always celebrate special dates and occasions. Our past broken marriages and failed relationships have taught us how to nurture and celebrate our love without smothering our individual needs.

My ideal relationship isn't necessarily right for everyone. I know a multimillionaire whose goals and achievements destroyed his marriage. His priorities left no time for his family, but that was his choice. Without making a value judgment, I was curious to know how he managed his social life, for he dated many attractive, interesting women. He usually treated them to a wonderful evening. Sometimes he, or his secretary, sent flowers or a gift. Although he is now in his sixties, he is still attractive, sexually active, and relatively uninvolved. When his marriage collapsed he decided that he would continue to enjoy an active social and sex life but refrain from entering a long-term relationship that could lead to a commitment. He is in control of his emotions and does not let emotional matters interfere with his objectives. His style of dealing with emotions may be too programmed for you or me, but he decided how he would handle his emotional life, and apparently it works for him.

◆ Does Your Romance Enhance?

Love can inspire, stimulate, and enrich our lives. We all need loving relationships; we need to have fun, share feelings and dreams. The happiest high achievers I talked with worked hard to have a stable, nurturing, fulfilling love relationship. Some had long, rich marriages. But there were a striking number of second marriages or live-in arrangements. Batik artist Sara Eyestone, mother of four from a previous marriage, is deliriously happy with her second husband, who has his own career but is very much involved in promoting Sara's work.

Bronnie Kupris, mother of two teenagers, founder of the Gallery of Wearable Art and president of Asti Tours, Inc., in New York, attributes much of her success to her "lifeline," the love of her life who solidly supports whatever she does and loves her like crazy.

Steve Burzon, father of two sons and publisher of *Metropolitan Home* magazine, is still aglow from his recent second marriage. He and his wife, a successful career woman, have found the right combination of together and apart.

Your love life can bring you deep satisfaction, fulfillment, and pleasure. You can shape your love relationship into a beautiful source of creativity, renewal, and bountiful caring, growing closer to others and the ultimate fulfillment of life.

Decide if your romantic life is fueling your growth and achievement or if it is sapping your vital energy, wasting your time, and distracting you from your goals.

◆ *How Does Your Emotional River Flow?*

Think of your emotions as an underground river that ebbs and flows, with temperatures that change from cold to warm to hot. When there are no mountain springs, no outlets for continuous release, pressure builds until a geyser spews forth. When anger turns your underground streams to lava, there had better be ways of defusing the pressure or a violent volcano is certain to erupt. Fear flows both icy cold and scalding hot and can pollute the other emotions. From the warm, gentle waters of love spring sparkling fountains, showering your world with euphoria, sometimes distorting reality and dissipating the desire for achievement.

Study your underground emotional currents and temperatures. Don't let them burst into floods that wipe out your sense of purpose and commitment to your goals. Don't spend your valuable time cleaning up the mud and emotional debris left in the wake of a tidal wave of uncontrolled emotions.

◆◆

◆ *Check Your Anger Currents*
· Accept the fact that you will be angry sometimes.
· Recognize anger. Know that you are feeling it when you are mad.
· Get it out. Find a release that fits the occasion.
· Cultivate regular activities that are good for letting off steam.

◆ *Accept Your Fears*
· Uncover the fears in your life.
· Admit it when you're afraid.
· Don't let fear stop you from getting what you want out of life.
· Stay with your goals even if it means enduring fear.

· Battling with fear and winning brings a new freedom, confidence, and clear sailing toward your goals.

◆ *Take Your Love Temperature*
· Don't be a "love junkie."
· Don't use love as an excuse or an escape.
· Take charge of your romantic emotions.
· Decide what kind of relationship is right for you.
· Build a relationship that nurtures, restores, and renews, that allows personal growth along with the special rewards of sharing.

◆◆

11

◆

Opportunity Seldom Knocks

I am not surprised at what men suffer,
but I am surprised at what men miss.

—JOHN RUSKIN

LIKE MILLIONS OF people I grew up with the old adage "Be ready, for you never know when opportunity will knock." That led me to believe that someone would hear about my efforts, and that because I was a nice person they would give me a call or write me a letter offering me the chance of a lifetime. That may happen in a few cases, but I've found that if opportunity has to knock, it's too late. Chances are it knocked on every other door on the block and got rejected! Do you want other people's cast-off opportunities? If you wait for the old "outside force," you could be passing up that chance of a lifetime and maybe *waiting* a lifetime.

Here's what I've learned about opportunity:

1. Opportunity wears disguises and hides in unlikely places.
2. Opportunity can be created from a mere wisp of an idea, not necessarily your own.
3. Opportunities must be carefully analyzed before you commit yourself to them . . . do your homework!

4. Opportunities can be exploited to bring fantastic rewards!
5. Opportunity is different from money.

◆ *How Do You Recognize Opportunity?*

Opportunities can occur in some of the most unlikely places. One of the more interesting assignments I had while hosting the *In Person* program in Cincinnati was to interview an "exotic dancer." I'm sure I didn't fool the viewer for a second. Everyone knows "exotic dancer" means stripper, but it sounded more polite in the script. We arranged to do our videotaping at the Brass Ass (I said "Brass Mule" in the script), a nightclub in Newport, Kentucky. Although Newport was once a wide-open river town, the nightlife had long since settled down, but there was still plenty of action for our purposes. I was more than curious about my guest, Sheri Lee. Since she worked a different "shift" from mine, I had to set the alarm for 2:00 A.M. to reach her at work so we could arrange the details of the taping. I explained that we would do the interview sitting on the stage before the club's patrons arrived. We also asked that she change costumes and go through a routine or two for a sample of her work.

I had been sheltered from this sort of thing, so I wasn't completely comfortable in that environment. My little gray blazer and matching scarf just heightened my "uptight" look. Everything went beautifully, however. Sheri put me at ease immediately. She was young, pretty, very wholesome looking, and she talked of her young daughter. She could have been my neighbor in the subdivision. Her husband, a former stunt actor, was her manager and he explained that they led a relatively normal life. We all got along famously. Sheri invited me to her dressing room to show me her expensive costumes and how they were designed to come off on stage. We posed for publicity pictures together on the club's stage. As we were wrapping up the night's work, Sheri's manager-husband drew me aside and quietly remarked, "You know, you have thin ankles. That's essential to be a success in this business. Listen, how much do they pay you at that TV station? You could do well in this business. Here's my card. Think about it, and give me a call if you ever get bored and want to make a name for yourself."

At the time I did not recognize that offer as an opportunity. It was outrageous, but I was secretly flattered. For a while my favorite one-liner became "Well, if this doesn't work, I can always be a stripper!"

Another interesting opportunity occurred after the Miss America Pageant. A talent scout invited me to come to New York and join the chorus line of a new Broadway show, *The Night They Raided Minsky's*. My parents were appalled at the idea, and I wanted to get married and raise a family after college graduation. It was an opportunity quickly rejected, and given another chance, I would probably turn it down again. But how can we have any control over such possibilities if we don't recognize them as true opportunities? How can we be open for those expanding and enlightening experiences when we have not even seen half of the ones that passed by?

In *The Money Personality*, psychiatrist Dr. Sidney Lecker stresses that one of the most important attributes needed for success is "being able to see big opportunities in little things. . . . Lucrative business deals are like gold—you find them in the dirt."

Develop your opportunity antenna. Pick up the beams of opportunity that may be invisible to the naked eye. Don't make opportunity hit you over the head before you see it. Listen for opportunity possibilities during conversations. As you read newspapers and magazines, be open to opportunity ideas. Listen to the musings of friends and associates. Be aware of the obvious. Sometimes opportunities are so obvious you may not recognize them.

Back in the 1940s, Dale Nelson was a salesman for a floor-care products company. Day in and day out he saw that most of the commercial cleaning services in Des Moines, Iowa, were small mom-and-pop operations. He was convinced that he could establish a more consistent, professional operation. Today, Dale Nelson's Building Maintenance Service, Inc., employs five hundred with annual sales of more than $4 million.

Nelson picked up an opportunity I knew about but didn't

pursue. When I was a full-time homemaker I constantly heard my friends complain about the lack of professional cleaning help, the inferior training or unreliable approach to household maintenance support. After my own experience with unreliable and disappointing cleaning help, I became more certain that there was a thriving business opportunity there. It was a super opportunity then, and it still is an opportunity that exists in towns and cities across America.

Test everything you see, hear, and read for opportunity clues. Put up your opportunity antenna for hidden possibilities. There may be one right in your own living room. Sue Garland, who lives outside Washington, D.C., was laid off her job as a high school teacher. While looking for other work, she supported herself as a private tutor. She recognized an opportunity when she heard parents repeatedly ask if she knew of tutors who taught other subjects. From her dining room table Sue started Traveling Tutors, a service that provides tutoring in all subjects for all educational levels through College. That was eight years ago. Now Traveling Tutors employs two hundred tutors and five additional full-time employees.

Five years ago, when Katherine Diamond's two sons were still in school, she applied for a job at a commercial language center. Although she'd had previous experience as a language instructor and interpreter, she was offered only $4.80 an hour. Instead she developed a business plan and located instructors in fifty different languages. In January 1980, Katherine opened Language Learning Enterprises from her living room. Last year she grossed $250,000, and her client list includes the foreign service, Visa, Comsat, and other major corporations.

Opportunities seldom start out big. Like Sue Garland and Katherine Diamond, you may have to look in the corners for little ones, too. Dr. Sidney Lecker found a man who became a billionaire from producing the little valves used in aerosol spray cans. I know a multimillionaire who manufactures and distributes one product—the small order pads used by waiters and waitresses in restaurants.

In many cases getting fired means opportunity. That was

how it happened with Gerry Hanus when he lost his job with
E. F. Hutton. He took $396 from his savings and began de-
signing furniture in his garage that "meets an unsatisfied
sector of the market, and offers good quality at a modest
price." Everyone thought Gerry was crazy. His parents told
him to get back in a "regular" job, but he has stayed with his
plan since 1975. In 1982, Gerry's company, Contemporary
Comforts, sold seven million dollars' worth of furniture! Look
around . . . opportunities are there!

◆ Create Opportunity!

One of the best ways to discover opportunity is to explore your own mind. Gerry Hanus, the man who started
Contemporary Comforts furniture, had no background in
manufacturing or design. His field was finance, but he got the
idea of creating a furniture company. His idea became the
opportunity that paid off in the millions and brought new
recognition.

I recently met Earle Swensen, who heads the famous
Swensen Ice Cream Company, with ice cream parlors bearing
his name all across the country. He is in his seventies, looks
very prosperous, and at a glance you might wonder if Swensen
inherited the company. Mr. Swensen agreed to appear as my
guest on *Today* to personally assemble a special Fourth of
July Sundae with scoops of red, white, and blue ice cream.
Such a segment was bound to get tricky. It takes a few minutes to get the microphones hooked on and get comfortable
on the set, and I like to talk through the sequence of a dem-
onstration on the set with the props just before we go "on."
It relaxes the guest and gives him a chance to know what it
will feel like when we do it live. The ice cream presented
some obvious problems. We talked through the action with
the ice cream and had time to spare. As I watched Mr. Swensen grow more and more nervous while red, white, and blue
ice cream melted to a pale lavender, I made an attempt at
casual conversation by asking, "How did you get in this
business, anyway?" In the two minutes we had to wait, he
told me this story.

Earle Swensen was stationed on a troop ship during

World War II. According to Earle, the sailors on board the ship thought about three things—women, hamburgers, and ice cream, in that order. So he used to enjoy going down to the galley to help make ice cream for the five thousand men on the ship. It seems that the ice cream they made wasn't that good, but "it was cold, and it was the idea they liked as well as anything."

After the war, Earle landed a good civil service job, and he and his wife, Nora, settled down for a long, secure life in the San Francisco area. But the recollection and satisfaction of making ice cream stayed with Swensen, so one day he quit his job, took his last $700, and he and Nora started the Swensen Ice Cream Company. Today there are 360 Swensen Ice Cream Parlors, with expansion plans on the horizon.

Earle Swensen did not go on an opportunity "hunt," and he didn't know about market research or "networking." His opportunity came from his own mind—the memories and fascination he had for ice cream.

Bronnie Kupris was another of my Lifestyle guests who created her own opportunity. She appeared on *Today* as an expert on "wearable art," hand-made, one-of-a-kind garments that could truly be considered art. Ms. Kupris really did not need an opportunity for personal growth and achievement, for she had inherited a successful travel agency, Asti Tours, from her mother. Bronnie told me how at one point she was advised to shut down or sell the travel agency, invest the revenue in secure, tax-free securities, and live very comfortably for the rest of her life. Although Bronnie is the consummate, high-energy high achiever, she saw the wisdom of settling down to a carefree existence.

But Bronnie had a lifelong burning interest in hand-made, artistic, custom-designed clothing. Wherever she traveled, she looked for those special treasures, and consequently she accumulated an extraordinary collection. Bronnie did her homework and decided to keep the travel agency business, take her "security" money, and open the Gallery of Wearable Art in the SoHo district of Manhattan. During the three-hour gala opening Bronnie did $7,000 worth of business, and she was not yet officially open for business! On Saturdays you will find customers lined up outside her shop waiting for a chance to try on the unique garments and wearable accessories. Important artists compete for a spot in her store gallery, and boutiques in other cities have urged Bronnie to start a wholesale distribution business. Tour buses unload their curious out-of-towners at the door of the gallery while Bronnie watches her special dream become a reality. She didn't have to look far for her opportunity . . . it had been her hobby for years.

What are your secret desires? What are your interests and hobbies? What do you really like to do? Your opportunity may be right in your own mind and soul.

◆ Analyze Opportunities . . . It Pays to Do Your Homework

It is not hard to discover inspirational-opportunity stories, and it's not difficult to find the opportunities. Unfortunately, opportunity does not appear with a "go" or "no go" sign. That's for you to figure out. It's true, opportunities can change your life and lead you closer to your goals, even achieve your goals, but like risks they require careful consideration and analysis. Sometimes the thrill of discovering an opportunity can sweep you into a commitment before you have carefully weighed all the angles. The get-rich-quick salesmen are masters of promising huge returns on little investments to the opportunity-starved novice. The best rule is to think carefully: never plunge ahead immediately with *any* new opportunity, even if it's one of those famous "sure-fire ideas" that can't fail. Even if it has been a hobby or you have been working on it part-time, always invest the necessary time and effort to examine every aspect of the opportunity. Do your homework! Each of the high achievers in this chapter made sure their opportunities would work!

Have you ever heard of Bear Archery? It's one of the most respected names in sport and hunting bows. Sixty years ago Fred Bear took a job at the Packard auto plant in Detroit. In the evenings he made bows in his garage. For ten years he built bows as a hobby before he quit his job at the auto plant to incorporate his new business. Current estimated annual sales of Bear Archery top $20 million, but like most high achievers Bear isn't in it for the money. What was his success strategy? As he told *Nation's Business* magazine, he wanted a business that did not take too much time, so he could go hunting and fishing whenever he wanted; he researched his potential market carefully and discovered that in 1933 there were no companies doing what he proposed; and he wanted satisfying work, something he liked to do. He saw the opportunity that could achieve his goals. He also correctly predicted that bow hunting would become enormously popular. Now it has grown into a major competitive sport.

You can find your dream opportunity, but test the waters first. Do your homework. Find out about the competition and how much time, specialized expertise, and money it will take to begin. Use your risk-taking skills to avoid disappointments and setbacks. The right opportunity can make you a success story.

◆ Exploit Opportunities

Eight years ago Joe Bahnatka was teaching social studies; Joe's wife was a secretary. They both really wanted to go into some business together, but what business? They heard about a convalescent-supply firm in another state and became interested when they realized that there was nothing like it in their area. The Bahnatkas spent a year researching it before they decided to do it. At first it was only a part-time business; they stored the necessary wheelchairs, walkers, and hospital beds in their garage. It was a perfect arrangement, for Joe's wife, Dot, could manage the business while staying at home with the children, and Joe could make deliveries after school and in the evenings. But Medicare took off, and Joe and Dot were soon devoting themselves full-time to the business. Last year sales reached $2.5 million, up 50 percent from the year before.

The Bahnatkas spent a year researching the business, then committed only part-time efforts, but once they realized the business was viable Joe quit teaching and they made a full-time commitment.

Once you have determined that your opportunity is a

winner, go for it! Don't be an "opportunity collector" with frustrated, regretful tales of the ones that "got away." Commit yourself to it, and make it work! The people in this chapter are real people, like you and me. Frankly, I'm tired of the excessive media attention given to the phenomenal success stories of Mrs. Fields Cookies and Mary Kay Cosmetics; I'm not looking for "media blitz" success stories; and stories of Thomas Edison and Henry Ford have worn thin. I want to know how the unassuming "little guy" does it today!

Exploiting opportunities, really making them work for you, draws on many of the high-achiever skills discussed earlier in this book. In fact, you may be hearing echoes of earlier themes. For example:

1. Test all your risk-taking skills. In fact, many opportunities present major risks, and they should be handled as risks.

2. Exploiting an opportunity tests your persistence, resilience, and ability to work hard and reinforce your inner steel.

3. An opportunity means a challenge. Will you accept the challenge?

4. Opportunities may be visualized or encouraged by applying your powers of visualization.

5. Opportunity may require you to "be a learner" and do the necessary homework in order to make the right choice.

6. An opportunity may require you to "give yourself permission." Remember Gerry Hanus, whose parents urged him to find "regular" work and whose friends told him he was crazy? He had to give himself permission to pursue his opportunity.

7. Opportunity asks us to "have faith in failure." No matter how sure the plan, or the amount of homework and research, problems can occur. But feeling confident in the face of setbacks is a tremendous advantage.

Find opportunities or create them. Learn to recognize them, and identify the ones that fit your master goal plan.

When you seize an opportunity that can bring you closer to your goal, exploit it—go for it! Opportunities can speed you on your way and bring surprise bonus benefits.

♦ *Opportunity* vs. *Money*

A curious thing happens on the way to success. For the high achiever money is seldom the motivating factor. When faced with the choice of money or opportunity, most high achievers chose opportunity without hesitation. Then, almost miraculously, the money started to abundantly flow. In several of the cases I discussed, the people actually gave up jobs and their security to exploit an opportunity.

Big money was not the goal. Earle Swensen really *wanted* to make ice cream. Gerry Hanus *wanted* to try his hand at exploiting a segment of the furniture market. Sue Garland, who founded Traveling Tutors, really *wanted* to teach. Sure, these people needed to earn a living, and I'm sure they would prefer to have more money than not enough, but that wasn't the reason for their accomplishment. In most of the cases, increasing their wealth was a secondary consideration, and when the money began to roll in they were pleasantly surprised. As I have found in many cases, the payoff for high achievers who recognize their goals exceeds their wildest expectations.

♦ *Opportunity Pays*

Of course, it would be naive not to consider the income possibilities when analyzing an opportunity or risk. But beware of making money the primary consideration. As P. T. Barnum said, "Money is in some respects like fire . . . it is a very excellent servant but a terrible master. When you have it mastering you . . . it will keep you down in the worst kind of slavery."

Money is also an elusive goddess. Just when you think you finally have your fill of money and "things," something newer, brighter, better, more exclusive, a new and more seductive trinket appears on the horizon just out of reach, diminishing the satisfaction of your most recent acquisition.

It's a cruel cycle. The pursuit of money alone is a hollow goal that can breed insatiable appetites, discontent, and greed.

Dr. Gerald Kushel, author of *Centering,* explains that one of the major obstacles that can stand in the way of clarifying your passionate purposes is the "illusion that the pursuit of more money is a valid end in itself."

Granted money is the standard measure of success in this country. For some, the struggle to succeed grows out of not having enough—that "standing outside looking in" feeling of not being able to afford certain clothes, cars, or the luxury extras. Money is the tangible reward for our efforts. It's obvious we can't carry around our diplomas, awards, or children, but we can show off expensive cars, diamonds, furs, and a fresh suntan from Costa del Sol.

It's easy to see how goals can be misdirected toward money. All around us there is pressure to have, make, spend, save, caress money. Money is laden with emotional baggage, it confuses our very identity, or lovability. It can become a form of expression or a dangerous weapon of control and suppression. It has been the undoing of many talented in dividuals, and it has shattered families and brought misery and pain to others . . . not because money itself is a destructive force, but because of the way we perceive and use money.

As Dr. Gerald Kushel states, "Money is power . . . but if you have plenty of personal power . . . money becomes proportionately less important to you."

The most contented, fulfilled achievers seem to have a relaxed attitude toward money. It is not their driving force. If you set goals that are truly your personal desires, the money tends to take care of itself.

My first job in television in Lincoln, Nebraska, paid only $5 a show. Twelve years later in Cincinnati the job hosting *In Person* paid only $11,500 a year. I started on *A.M. Buffalo* at $20,000 a year, which seemed like a fortune to me since it was nearly double my pay in Cincinnati. After my interview for the *Today* position, the executive producer apologetically told me the job "didn't really pay anything." Actually it more than doubled my Buffalo salary, and now after four years my earnings have moved into six figures! I never imagined I would ever earn so much money. But that's not why I worked so hard. My motivation was the challenge, the thrill of accomplishment, the prospect of working with other high achievers, the stimulation of growth, the exhilaration of watching my own ideas form visual information to be shared with millions of viewers.

The theme of challenge and growth recurs among the many high achievers I have observed and questioned. When I ask, "How does it feel to be so rich?" over and over I hear, "Oh, I'm not in this just for the money. It's nice to have the things I want, but I really love doing what I'm doing." Every high achiever I interviewed or studied chose opportunity over money.

Another common response indicated a true liberation from the money trap: "If I lost it all today, I know that I could start all over and make it work again." That's the kind of inner confidence that no money can buy.

◆◆◆

Here are some ways to make opportunity a part of your achievement program:

- Look for opportunities all around you—in conversations and in what you read, do, and buy.
- Create opportunities of your own. Use your imagination, consider your hobbies, the things you love to do.
- Do your homework before committing to a new opportunity. Be sure it's the one you want.
- Move in on opportunities—do it. Don't let your chance of a lifetime fly by.
- Don't get seduced by money. Go after your opportunity and trust that the money will follow.

◆◆◆

Become an alert opportunity watcher!

12

♦

Take Good Care
of Yourself

---

*Self-neglect is a form of suicide, a first
step in the destruction of one's nature.*

—DAVID SEABURY, The Art of Selfishness

♦ *Your Health and Fitness*

I was over thirty when I learned to ski. You may recall
from an earlier chapter how frightened I was of the lifts, the
hard falls, and the sheer speed of my unprotected body hurling
down an icy mountain. I had been fairly nonathletic all my
life, and the prospect of breaking my bones, biting off a chunk
of my tongue, or suffering a heart attack from the stark terror
of the slopes loomed in my mind. As a young teacher in
Colorado after college I had known a member of the ski patrol
who had generously (and graphically) shared all the gruesome
events of midmountain rescues and the perils of the Vail,
Colorado, hospital emergency room. Certainly I wanted to
spare myself and my family the inconvenience (to say nothing
of my discomfort) that "a mommy disability" would cause.
Besides, crutches were not my favorite wardrobe accessory!

Up until that time I had been active, but only in the day-
to-day demands of home and family. To me fitness meant that
I could wear a size six or eight dress. However, my fear of
the ski slopes and the thinner air of the Rocky Mountains

pushed me to get in shape for my first encounter with a new and potentially dangerous sport as an "older person." (That's how "over thirty" felt then.) For three months prior to the ski trip I jogged the half-mile lane to the mailbox and back, instead of driving. I wanted to increase my lung capacity and endurance, as well as build strength in my legs. For two months I jogged and performed several exercises I saw in *Ski* magazine. The most wonderful thing happened. I began to feel better than ever. I had more energy, I didn't get as tired, I slept better, I was much less nervous, I'd lost some flabby spots, and I just had a greater sense of well-being. The preparation for skiing paid off. While others were huffing and puffing in the thin mountain air, I was more stable and had no trouble keeping up with the "younger" class members in strength or endurance.

The pre–ski trip fitness program was the beginning of a fitness habit that will be with me my whole life. It helped me immeasurably during times of pressure, and it has become an integral part of my daily routine.

My fitness and nutrition program developed gradually to suit my needs. I was hardly aware that it was becoming a national pastime. Now diet and fitness are big business in America. While Americans are in better health than ever before, and there is a growing awareness of personal responsibility to maintain one's health, market research indicates that there is still an alarming collective need to look to an outside method of imposing effective diet and fitness habits. Each month brings a new book on diet with its promises and programs, some kind of new gimmick diet that's the last word on weight loss. It's the same with exercise. We have aerobics, Dancercise, spot exercise, Heavyhands, and gravity boots. Again, whether we're tugging, pulling, stretched, prodded, or inverted, we are looking for some outside force to impose the discipline, assume the responsibility, provide us with the answers.

Many people get stuck in the fitness trap, making diet and exercise a goal instead of a means to an end. The idea of taking control of your health is to increase your energy, improve your appearance, confidence, and feeling of well-being in order to reach your goals—to promote growth, to enable you to better manage the challenges of achievement. Fitness should not be an end in itself, unless, of course, you have aspirations as a serious marathoner, health-club manager, or Olympic competitor. Keep your diet and fitness in perspective. It is important, but let it work *for* you instead of dominating your whole sense of purpose.

As Lifestyle correspondent, I see most of the new diet and exercise books and programs since they pass through my office. Many "experts" in the field have appeared on *Today.* I consider most of the "here today, gone tomorrow" diet and fitness programs to be the product of skillful promotion rather than sound advice. In the hands of professional "hype masters," these trendy programs simply exploit our own laziness, ignorance, or insecurity, while making a few publishers and packagers richer.

Developing and maintaining a personal program of diet and fitness is not that complicated, and after reading stacks of books on the subject and conducting interviews with "experts," I can honestly say that whatever exercise you need can be done in or around your own home without expensive equipment. The only thing you need to develop a sound, weight-conscious nutritional program is a comprehensive calorie chart and a small food scale. When you discover that one tablespoon of margarine is 100 calories, you begin to watch what you put on salads and vegetables. If a slice of bread is 100 calories, a sandwich is 200 without the filling. For a lark I bought a small food scale no bigger than a coffee mug. What a surprise it was to actually see the size of a four-ounce pork cutlet or hamburger, or two ounces of cheese. Most of us eat portions that are much too big. Once you become aware of basic calorie load and portion sizes, it becomes automatic mental math.

You don't need to be an expert to learn what makes you feel your best. Whose body is it, anyway? Who is best qualified to know what's best for you? Go ahead and accept the responsibility for your daily nutrition and fitness! Wonderful things happen when you do.

Oddly enough, the very people you might expect would

be too busy to maintain a regular health program are the ones who make it a priority. According to a survey conducted by Howard-Sloan, Inc., the Fortune 500 chief executive officers, who have severe time limitations, "exercise regularly, watch their diets, have a low incidence of hypertension, and get at least six hours of sleep every night." Stephen Berger, president of the firm that conducted the survey, was not surprised by the results. He observed, "These people have everything in good order. They enjoy work and the challenge it presents. They work more than other people, yet [they] manage to maintain good health habits."

A growing number of U.S. corporations are learning that not only the employee, but the entire company benefits from a regular fitness program. Many companies have installed in-house fitness centers to be used on company time to encourage optimum performance, reduce the number of sick days, prevent employee "burnout," and promote the fitness habit.

The Sentry Corporation got involved in company fitness in a big way. Sentry's $3 million "wellness center" includes an indoor gymnasium, an Olympic-size pool, Nautilus equipment, and a quiet lounge for meditation or rest breaks. Use of Sentry's facilities is not limited to executives. Recently, Richard Novak, Sentry's fifty-five-year-old treasurer, explained, "I started running to get in shape for the hunting season and it felt so good I didn't stop. You feel better about yourself, and as a result, you work better with others."

It really works. To learn and grow and be challenged, to reach for higher goals, to take risks and work hard, to endure setbacks and still bounce ahead, to live life to the fullest requires the optimum performance of body and mind. You must take care of yourself!

John Naisbitt, author of *Megatrends,* made several appearances on *Today,* exploring his massive research on American habits, life-styles, and future social trends. In the area of personal health he concluded:

> A basic wellness movement is simple and un-
> controversial: regular exercise, no smoking,
> a healthy diet with low to moderate intake

of fat, salt, sugar, and alcohol, adequate rest,
and stress control. Personal habits are the key
element in the new health paradigm, so personal responsibility is critical.

My own diet and fitness program is a continuing process
requiring frequent adjustments and fine-tuning according to
the signals I receive from my body and mind. When I first
saw myself on camera I was startled to see that I looked
heavier. Later I discovered that everyone looks around ten
pounds heavier when they appear on camera, so I made an
effort to take off a few pounds. However, when I meet someone who has only seen me on television he or she invariably says,
"You look so much thinner in person!"

My own philosophy of health and fitness matches that
of Drs. Harold Bloomfield and Robert Kory in *The Holistic
Way to Health and Happiness:* "You must look at all parts of
yourself—body, mind, spirit and environment—as an organic
whole and determine what elements are out of balance. Your
eating habits, nutrition, emotions, physical fitness and exercise routine, stress level, work or home environment, and even
your sense of meaning and purpose in life must be taken
into account."

Diet and exercise have become integrated in my normal
daily routine and in my overall attitude toward maintaining
health. In fact, it has become so automatic that it takes some
effort to isolate the main points:

1. I find that most people don't drink enough water. I try
   to drink seven glasses of water a day. I drink the first
   glass the moment I get up in the morning. Adequate
   water promotes weight control, helps keep the energy
   level high, and is critical for healthy skin.

2. A brisk walk or jog four to five times a week is essential,
   more if weather and schedules permit. The distance
   varies between one-half to two miles.

3. I do ten to twenty minutes of stretching and bending
   exercises, including special exercises for areas that may
   need extra work (tummy, sides, thighs).

4. I get eight hours of sleep at night—difficult, but essential.
5. I always eat breakfast, even if it's only juice and cereal or toast. No junk foods—potato chips, Twinkies, and the like. I avoid red meat. My diet includes lots of fresh fruits and vegetables, whole grains, a glass of wine three or four times a week with the evening meal. I limit salt, potatoes, and fancy desserts. I stop eating before I feel full. I never eat or drink anything right before bedtime.

I don't feel in the least deprived. We have delicious, simple meals that fuel our high-energy needs. Once the natural balance of the body is established, it isn't difficult to stick with the program. I wouldn't think of eating a potato chip or the rich hors d'oeuvres at parties. Whatever fleeting gratification I might get, it's simply not worth jeopardizing the balance of my system. Consequently, I have no trouble passing them up.

For fear of sounding like a born-again "health nut," let me quote Dr. Lester Breslow, dean of the UCLA School of Public Health. He conducted a survey of seven thousand California adults, and found these seven basic living habits "crucial to good health":

1. No smoking
2. Moderate drinking
3. Seven to eight hours of sleep nightly
4. Regular meals with no between-meal snacking
5. Breakfast every day
6. Maintain normal weight
7. Moderate, regular exercise

There are no surprises here, just as there are no magic tricks in my own diet and fitness program. It's just a matter of taking charge and giving yourself the best treatment. You will soon begin to tune in to your body and feel what is best for your physical and mental well-being. Once you experience the extra energy, more youthful look and outlook, greater peace of mind, and confidence of being in control of your own fitness, you will never want to lose it! Tune your body for optimum performance, and feel the difference as you S-T-R-E-T-C-H toward your goals!

♦ *Alone to Yourself*

> I am here alone for the first time in weeks to take up
> my real life again at last.
>   —May Sarton
>   *Journal of a Solitude*

There is a wonderful story about a professor who became determined to learn everything he could about Zen. He went to speak to the most qualified Zen master, who began to pour tea while the professor rattled on about how much study he had done on the subject. The Zen master calmly continued to pour tea and kept pouring until the professor's teacup spilled over the saucer and all over the table. The professor jumped up and exclaimed, "The cup is overflowing." The Zen master replied, "Like your own mind, the cup is overfull. You must empty it before you can know Zen."

We don't have to go in search of Zen to appreciate the need to clear the mind. Another recurrent theme among high achievers is the need to regularly spend time alone. The amount of time seems to vary according to the individual and the type of work being done. It is well-known that Winston Churchill and Harry Truman used brief rest periods to sustain their energy and vitality. Among the high achievers I've talked with, many planned activities that provided time alone. Living a life devoted to achievement and growth, living life to the fullest, requires enormous energy, and even the best planning cannot reduce all the intensity that takes a toll on our physical and mental health. Having time alone is essential to maintain energy and restore a sense of calm and balance.

Spending time alone sounds like such a simple way to take care of yourself, but the majority of people go to great lengths to avoid being alone. Anne Morrow Lindbergh made this rich observation in *Gifts From the Sea*:

> We seem so frightened today of being alone
> that we never let it happen. Even if family,

friends and movies should fail, there is still
the radio or television to fill up the void. . . .
We choke off the space with continuous music, chatter and companionship to which we
do not even listen.

In *Centering,* Dr. Gerald Kushel has observed that one
of the major obstacles that can stand in the way of achieving
goals is "loneliness anxiety." Aloneness anxiety can block
achievement and the chance to realize the joy of a richer, more
peaceful existence.

I can usually tell when I need to spend time alone. When
I have been around people all day, and there has been too
much talking, too much traffic and noise, too many lists,
schedules, and deadlines, I grow tired, irritable, and edgy.
That tells me it's time to pull the plug. Often a quiet walk or
a drive alone offers a quick tranquillity fix. Sometimes spending a few minutes weeding a flower bed is all that's needed.
Some days closing the office door and listening to a few minutes of soothing music instantly restores inner calm and re-
charges the battery.

Being alone is nothing to fear. Quite the contrary, the
people to whom I spoke all looked forward to the few minutes
a day they had alone to themselves. Stephen Burzon, the in-
tensely creative, highly charged publisher of *Metropolitan
Home* magazine, uses his daily jog of five to seven miles to
commune with nature and himself. Author and filmmaker
Mel London sets aside ten days each February to retreat to the
family home on Fire Island alone. There he walks the desolate
cold beach, experiments with new recipes, catches up on reading, and thinks, alone.

Dianne Feinstein, mayor of San Francisco, is one of many
in high-stress work who advocate hydrotherapy. She says, "A
hot bath or even a shower will help erase the stress that results from hour-after-hour appointments and hassles." That's
something that not only brings the soothing effects of water,
but offers time alone.

Investment adviser John Templeton, founder of the super-
successful Templeton Group of mutual funds, went in for

time alone in a big way. To calm his thinking and gain perspective, he moved his whole operation to the Bahamas. He
spends at least an hour a day on the beach mulling over important decisions that he must make. Obviously, few people
pull up stakes and relocate to surroundings that are more
conducive to meditation. However, Templeton does recommend some type of personal retreat, some way of spending
time alone to draw energy and restore peace of mind, to gain
a sense of control that will carry you through the demands of
the day.

In *The Holistic Way to Health and Happiness* by Bloomfield and Kory, the authors point out that Maslow and
other well-known psychologists have "asserted that periods
of solitude are critical to the continued vitality and well-being
of the highly creative, self-actualizing person." Their studies
show that the "exceptionally healthy, self-actualizing" people,
although they tend to be more active, manage to take time
out for quiet solitude. Psychoanalyst Sacha Nacht states, "Human life needs at moments to steep itself in silence from
which it draws essential nourishment and in which it develops its deepest roots."

Many swear by certain systems of meditation. Others find
yoga brings them inner peace and "centering" solace. For
some, nature is the best place for solitude. And "nap time" is
essential for others. Whatever the method, the benefits are
undisputed.

Dr. Gerald Kushel describes the special experience of
time alone. "You will begin to experience your own unique
inner feelings, the insides of your body, more sensually, more
vitally. . . . It is alone that the most profound experiences in
life can be appreciated and subsequently shared."

Moustakis writes: "Loneliness, rather than separating the
individual or causing a break or division of self, expands
the individual's wholeness, perceptiveness, sensitivity, and
humanity."

Give yourself permission to spend some time alone each
day. Use the time to regenerate, relax, and restore inner calm.
It may be the time you choose for your visualization exercises,
feeling and picturing your goals. Perhaps it means a few quiet

minutes spent in an enjoyable solitary activity like constructing a model, playing a musical instrument, baking bread, or sewing.

Time alone gives your intuitions and subconscious thoughts the opportunity and space to surface. Create the climate of healing silence. Listen to what your body and mind tell you. They have powerful regenerative mechanisms, but they have to be heard and felt. Don't expect instant flashing signs in your mind. Be patient. Trust the inner tides to wash up a feeling of confidence and tranquillity, along with important ideas, revelations, and decisions.

You deserve the best! So as part of your personal health program, protect the special time you need for yourself alone. Go on a "mental vacation." It costs nothing, takes but a few minutes, and often has more restorative benefits than a week away.

1. Plan time to be alone each day—try for thirty minutes, but even ten minutes is worthwhile.
2. Keep out all distractions—people, phones, noises, all thoughts of the world and its demands.
3. Empty your mind. Use deep-breathing techniques (see the chapter on visualization), focus on your favorite, most peaceful scene—waves rolling up on a beach, a tranquil lake, a fragrant garden of roses, or your favorite scents and textures.
4. Return to your routines refreshed, revitalized, and peaceful.

In addition to the concentrated solitude of your ten to thirty minutes alone, plan solitary activities that reinforce the regenerative rewards of time alone.

1. Use your jogging or exercise time to be alone.
2. Begin a hobby that is enjoyed only alone—reading, playing a musical instrument, building models, learning a computer program, needlepoint.
3. Insist that friends and family members allow you to do

certain activities alone—gardening, lawn care, flower arranging, evening walks, painting or sketching.
4. Recognize your symptoms of "solitude starvation"—feeling tense and irritable, constantly distracted—and get
away alone. Go for a walk, take a drive, go on a mental
vacation.

◆ What About Stress?

Perhaps it's just because I work in the media, but I have
developed a strong aversion to the word "stress." It really
means nothing except that something is out of balance and
needs attention. We picked up on stress and squeezed every
ounce of media juice out of it. We had stress tests, stress diets,
high-stress vitamins, antistress exercises and clinics, antistress
music and colors. I'm all stressed out! The fact is most high
achievers I've talked to have figured out how to take care of
themselves and have learned to listen to their own physical
and emotional needs. They can recognize the signals that call
for remedial activities and are never bothered by stress. But
what about the "type A personality"? Dr. Charles Garfield,
who is an extraordinary achiever himself and president of the
Peak Performance Center while concurrently a clinical professor at the University of California, insists that "super-
achievers are not workaholics or so-called type A executives.
High achievers take their vacations, relax at the end of the
day, don't get bogged down in details. Accordingly, they are
much less prone to heart attacks and the hazards of the type
A life-style."

Garfield supports my own observation that high achievers
strive to protect their health and maintain a balance in their
life that enables them to enjoy the fruits of their labor. There
is no longer any status associated with an ulcer or heart condition (if there ever was). I personally abhor the antacid commercials that assume that those late-night business meetings
around long conference tables always bring on stomach problems. I can't imagine that working overtime and sipping a
bitter antacid solution "for the symptoms that come with success" is the way most people want to live!

Let's take a minute for a backward glance at some of the

themes of earlier chapters. When you know what you want out of life and have decided on your goals; when you have learned to understand and harness emotions; when you know how to handle risks, challenges, and opportunities; when you know how to laugh at yourself and use humor to restore perspective; when setbacks can be turned into strengths; when you operate from an organized "lean machine"; and when you know how to take care of your health and psyche, there is no stress!

Take a moment to think of the beautiful symmetry of the interwoven themes of success. There is a balance and integration similar to nature itself. One of the ways to decode distress signals is simply to check through the list of chapters in this book. Pinpoint the area of dissatisfaction or weakness, and put extra effort into correcting the temporary malfunction. The secret is in maintaining and feeling a comfortable balance and integration of these forces. Believe me, it's worth the occasional fine-tuning, for you will reap immeasurable rewards in the quality of your life and a heightened appreciation of all that you experience.

◆ Reward Yourself

Early in my shaky career at WCPO-TV in Cincinnati, I was asked to fill in for a week as a substitute host of the Early 9 Movie, which aired each weekday afternoon between 4:00 and 6:00 P.M. *In Person* was a videotaped program; hosting the Early 9 Movie was live! The regular host must have been a frustrated game-show host, for he had invented an elaborate, electronic contraption with buttons, bells, and flashing lights that served as the set for the cut-ins during the movie breaks. But what was more dangerous was that it was also an attempt at some kind of game to keep viewers tuned in to the movie with the hope of winning that day's big "jackpot prize." The arrangement presented many problems. First, I considered the game corny (after all, I had Rosenthal china!), and it made me uncomfortable since it wasn't consistent with the solid professional image I was working to acquire. Second, I was inexperienced with even simple, live on-camera presentation; a complicated wall-sized board of switches and buttons could make a fool of me. Third, the whole situation could bring untold embarrassment to my family, because, as the boys moaned, "Ah, Mom, all the kids watch the Early 9 Movie. You're not going to tell jokes like Wirt Cane, are you?" And last, I could not refuse to accept this important opportunity for additional experience, since it was never exactly presented as an "invitation."

The week before I was to begin, my neck broke out in a blazing red rash just thinking about the Early 9 Movie, so I had to wear high neck scarves and turtlenecks the whole week of the debacle. As I recall, there was some kind of a "mystery celebrity" and a jackpot that could vary from ten to several hundred dollars. I had to explain the game, the mystery guest, and the jackpot at every movie break, dial at random a number from the Cincinnati phone book, be ready to deal with whomever and whatever was said, flash on the mystery guest, flash on the dollar sign, set off the whistle if there was a winner, and summarize the entire movie up to the break, all in two minutes! I was a wreck! But I did manage to muddle through without a major catastrophe. I didn't faint, start a fire, offend anyone on the phone, or humiliate the children. I was so relieved and exhilarated when that was over. Again, I'd learned another new skill on air!

I didn't expect any awards, but I was pleased that I got through the week unscathed. With the extra money earned from the ordeal I went to a local jewelry store and bought a lovely little diamond-and-ruby ring to symbolize an important accomplishment. I had prevailed in the storms of electronic buzzers and hungry live camera monsters. I could not expect anyone else to appreciate my victory. I was newly separated from my husband and needed to reward myself. The ring was an impulsive extravagance, but it started a very important habit in my life of celebrating the personal "quiet" victories. It doesn't have to be a ruby ring. What counts is that you take care of yourself by giving yourself well-deserved rewards. Don't look for praise and applause; you may not get them even when you most deserve it.

When we are children we constantly look to Mom or Dad for validation or praise. Watch children at the playground.

After every move they constantly glance back at Mom or Dad with that "Am I doin' okay?" look in their eyes. "Tell me I'm good . . . tell me I'm cute . . . look, Mom, no hands!" carries over to adulthood. While we may not return to our parents for approval, we do tend to need it from friends and colleagues. Some people crave praise and attention to the point of not being able to function well without it.

I remember one of my first lessons in the hard realities of depending on outside praise. After completing the grueling requirements of the audition at WCPO-TV I listened for applause, bravos, or just a simple "Nice job." I surprised myself that I got through it. But when the cameras shut off and the lights dimmed and I waited for the hugs and kisses, the lavish praise and congratulations, there was nothing. Silence. Instead, the crew wandered off for a cigarette break, and the normal postproduction routines resumed. Then the "voice" from the great nowhere, the unseen control room, boomed over the public-address system, "Thank you very much." That was it. Just "Thank you very much. . . ."

I should have been flattered. What I soon learned was that when you become a professional, exceptional performance is expected—in fact, it's taken for granted. That's what you're getting paid for.

Then and there I began to develop a process that I learned was common among high achievers. They develop an internal criteria, their own set of rules and standards, against which they measure their own performance and work. You begin to know what you are capable of doing. You know how to rate yourself. What others say about you and your work becomes less important. Your whole sense of professional pride does not depend on whether or not the "critics" gave you positive reviews, or any reviews at all.

Washington, D.C., psychologist Dr. Adi Shmueli explains that high achievers only validate and accept praise from other high achievers. They are the only ones who count—there is a mutuality, a feeling of being graded by an equal. But such peer "strokes" may be few and far between, for there is only a small chorus of other high achievers who appear from time to time to say, "Great job!" In the meantime, they all seem to do quite well without a lot of external approval or praise. Dr. Shmueli advises achievers to look for like achievers with whom to share feelings and rewards. It's marvelous when someone you respect and accept as an equal says, "I know how you feel." That is valid support and generally deeply appreciated.

Set up your own high standards and strive to perform according to your own internal criteria. Depend less on what others have to say about you and your work. Learn to recognize your own milestones, those accomplishments that may not mean a thing to anyone else. Not just the promotions and pay raises, but also the achievements that symbolize an important step in your growth. Maybe it's turning in a difficult report on time, losing the last ten pounds, completing a year as a club officer, or learning a new skill. Celebrate those important victories—even if they are private ones. It doesn't always have to be a purchase, although that tends to be my favorite. Here are a few ideas:

- Pick up a bottle of champagne and share it with a friend.
- Buy a new scarf or tie.
- Go out for a special dinner.
- Have a facial, manicure, massage, a good pampering.
- Break up the routine. Take the afternoon off! Go to the park, try something new, like flying a kite or fishing at noon.

Give yourself permission to reward yourself for a job well done. Look at it as a new entry in your journal of accomplishments.

Take care of yourself. You deserve the best!

◆◆

- For optimum performance, adopt a program of diet and fitness that is right for your physical, mental, and emotional needs. Integrate them into your daily routine so they become automatic.
- Spend some time alone each day.

  a. Give yourself a few minutes for quiet meditation.
  b. Devote some time to solitary activities.
  c. Plan an annual "retreat"—a few days completely
     alone, away from it all.
 · Be alert for symptoms that indicate something in your life
   is out of balance—irritability, overly impatient behavior,
   health problems—and make the necessary adjustments
   without delay.
 · Reward yourself! Don't wait for praise or recognition
   from others. Celebrate the private victories with special
   treats for you!

◆◆◆

Experience the joy and confidence that comes from good
physical and emotional health, the rejuvenation and renewal
that comes from having time alone, and the fun and heightened self-esteem that comes from knowing how to reward
yourself!

13

◆

Let Go of the Past

*There is grieving
to be done because an old self is dying.*
—GAIL SHEEHY, Passages

WHEN I WAS co-hosting *A.M. Buffalo,* EPA tests discovered that the Love Canal in Niagara Falls, New York, might be the center of life-threatening chemical contamination resulting from the burial of toxic waste materials. The Love Canal story erupted into a national controversy that raised environmental concern and alarm that continues to this day. Provisions were made to relocate families in the area believed to have been contaminated. For over a year, Love Canal was the top local news story. Among the many families to be relocated were a few who stubbornly held fast to their homes, refusing to leave the place that held so much of their past. The same thing occurred during the volcanic eruptions of Mt. Saint Helens in Washington. A number of families simply would not leave their homes. No amount of coaxing or court-ordering convinced them to evacuate, even if staying meant death. The general theme that ran through all the residents' comments seemed to be, "This is my house. I've spent most of my life here, and this is where I will stay." Even if the lava turned them to ashes! Surely that would be considered an irrational, even dangerous attachment to a physical symbol of the past.

There comes a time to move on. Fortunately, few of us are forced on by evacuation notices, but a little prodding now and then may prevent us from getting bogged down in the past. Staying in the same place, physically, emotionally, or intellectually, may be the easiest and most secure course, but it may not be the most direct route to our goals. In fact, it may not lead to our goals at all.

Early on, high achievers somehow develop a philosophy toward their past that allows them the freedom to grow beyond it while retaining the internal security it provides. Does your past have you on a short leash? Do you bound eagerly toward your goals only to be stopped short by your past? What is the "past"? The past can be old habits, attachments to possessions that no longer have relevance; people from the past who hold us back or stagnant relationships; even old guilt that binds and limits our growth.

◆ Letting Go

During the 1970s I was one of the thousands who faced the anguish of breaking with the past through the trauma of divorce. Except for the death of a loved one, divorce is probably the most shattering, tumultuous personal blow. Aside from the obvious emotional consequences, divorce forces us to let go of the past. The grieving, relocating, and being alone shattered me. Finally, nearly a year after the initial separation, I realized that my own dependence on the past was holding me back. I needed to do something concrete to demonstrate that I was disengaging emotionally.

Anyone who has been through a divorce knows there is an immediate change in the way your friends and associates relate to you. There is ambiguity, there are the inevitable questions ("What *really* happened?"), the address books are disrupted again, and who is going by which name? I needed to do something to help myself, and ultimately our friends, through the quagmire of marital "dissolution" with its rearranged people and feelings. We all know about marriage and birth announcements. I thought, why not a "dissolution announcement"? It would provide a clean statement of where we stand so we can get on with the final healing and the new life awaiting us—wherever it may be. I sent out the following:

April 1, 1978

WHAT?
Bill and Nancy have dissolved their marriage.
WHEN?
Initial separation occurred in late June 1977, and the final dissolution in late January 1978.
WHERE?
Nancy Foreman, and son Bill junior, 9, live at 000 Shady Meadow Drive, Princeton, New Jersey. Bill senior and son Jeff, 12, continue to reside at 000 Oakwood Drive, Cincinnati, Ohio.
NOW WHAT?
From January 1977 to January 1978, I anchored an interview program at WCPO-TV in Cincinnati. It was enriching, challenging, and provided an excellent foundation for my continuing career in television. While ending the marriage was difficult for us both, I must look ahead. I am currently employed by the television consulting firm of Roger B. Fransecky and Associates, Inc., with offices in Princeton and New York, while I seek a position with another television station.

The schools here are excellent and Bill junior has adjusted beautifully. Of course, Princeton University brings many cultural and educational advantages to this area. We enjoyed having Jeff with us for Easter, and look forward to seeing him again soon.

We need and appreciate our friends and their support, and would like to stay in touch.
Love,

Nancy Foreman   Bill, Jr.
(signed)   (signed)

I don't have to tell you how it felt to write that, or how many drafts I crumpled, or the number of Kleenex I soaked. But it forced me to deal with the finality of that chapter of my life. Few stages of growth are that traumatic, but there is a kind of grieving as we leave one stage and move on to the next.

Gail Sheehy helped millions sort through the normal confusion of growth in her best-selling book *Passages*. She explains:

> It would be surprising if we didn't experience some pain as we leave the familiarity of one adult stage for the uncertainty of the next . . . growth demands a temporary surrender of security. It may mean a giving up of familiar but limiting patterns, safe but unrewarding work, values no longer believed in, relationships that have lost their meaning.

There is sadness associated with moving on, but it helps to deal with it squarely. Admit the sadness, cry if you feel like it, write an announcement. There needn't be a divorce to announce change. Sometimes a clear statement of our status, whether in transition, redefined, or brand new, helps clarify and measure change for ourselves and others. In business, announcements regarding personnel changes and shifts in company policy are regularly circulated. By keeping change clearly defined, there is less chance of ambiguity, rumors, and staff anxiety.

Do you need to write a public or private change announcement? It doesn't have to be a mass mailer to help put the past in perspective. At the times of transition or change, those times when the past won't let go, try writing an announcement that clearly explains a change in your status. A clear declaration can bring a clear separation.

◆ The Stuff of Stagnation
Your old fishing hat, your First Communion dress, my little majorette boots, all had important meaning, and it is not

easy to toss out symbols of our former, younger selves. In chapter 9 ("The Lean Machine"), we talked about cleaning out the clutter for a simpler, smoother-running operation. We considered how life's accumulations can hold you back from an organizational point of view. Things from the past can weigh you down emotionally, too, and not simply in terms of tangible memorabilia. So much of what we carry with us we cannot see—it cannot be physically peeled away—but it looms just as formidably as the contaminated houses Love Canal's residents couldn't bear to leave. Doing a periodic cleaning of the attics of our past helps clear the way for achievement, growth, and a richer present.

◆ Old Habits for New Behavior

I still get nostalgic when something reminds me of my former self—the one who arranged dried flowers by the hour, hand-cut gingerbread men every Christmas, hand-dipped candles, and fringed placemats. Certain responses or habits can stubbornly persist when you really want to try out new behavior. For example, every time I see the price tag on a lovely arrangement of dried flowers, I instantly think, "What! Forty-five dollars! I could make that for a third of the price." My new self has to remind my old self that I've given up flower arranging, at least for now.

Another old habit that plagued me was the alterations situation. Every dress or skirt I buy has to be shortened. Consequently, I have known how to fix a hem since I was nine. When I moved to New York I was horrified to find that it cost twelve dollars to shorten a single hemline! I stubbornly declared that I would do it myself—"on the weekend." That "weekend" never came, and ankle-length skirts began to collect in the closet. Finally, I really needed the clothes and I ended up taking them all out at once to a neighborhood tailor; I paid a horrendous alterations bill. With the demands of my job and family, I had to face the fact that I could not continue to be my past and present selves at the same time.

As Gail Sheehy states, "If we don't change, we don't grow. If we don't grow, we are not really living." So what's the option? Stagnation, or worse? As my father's friend Gorman

King declares, "The only difference between a rut and a grave are the dimensions." It's impossible to accelerate into an exciting future with one foot stuck in the past.

Give yourself permission to let go of the past. Be prepared for a few tugs, especially around the holidays when someone passes the homemade cookies, when you have to pay for something that you used to do for yourself, or when the Goodwill truck rolls around to pick up the broken-down wicker furniture that so brightly furnished your first apartment.

◆ Shed the Clingers

Letting go of the places and things of the past is tough enough. Unfortunately, people can hold you back, too. Not everyone will celebrate your erratic growth cycles. Not everyone will understand or welcome the "new phase" of you. What about the people—the friends, neighbors, family members, and others—whom you discover would rather keep you the same? What happens when you don't have the time or energy to spend with those who have become accustomed to your attention? They can hold on tight. Your new priorities may not include sending out two hundred hand-made Christmas cards or giving forty-three personally selected and crafted gifts. You may not have the time to entertain and be entertained. Your rainy Sunday afternoons may become "organization" times, and there is no time to write the newsy family letters. There may no longer be time to hang on the telephone, passing on gossip or rehashing the past. Letting go of the past may mean rearranging, reordering, recasting your relationships.

You may be surrounded by "clingers" and not even know it. You may wonder why you are not moving ahead as consistently as you had hoped, why you are depleted of energy and time, or why you sometimes feel depressed, resentful, or guilty at the end of the day. You may be suffering from an overload of clingers!

First, you need to be able to recognize those "clingers." I've devised four categories, but you may be able to come up with several more of your own.

PARASITES: These are probably the most obvious. They

are blatantly concerned with meeting their own needs with no consideration for yours. They take more than they give and expect your generosity of time, ideas, whatever you have that they want, for they feel that your enhanced responsibility, expertise, and income entitle them to their portion. They will take advantage of you and count on your feelings of responsibility and guilt to come through with whatever they want.

MANIPULATORS: These guys are cagey. They recognize your talents and abilities, and much like the parasites, they want to own a share of them. They want to bask in your light without paying the electric bill. If you're not careful, they can derail you by constantly bending the nicely laid tracks to your goals. The new route will lead back to their agenda, not yours. They may offer ideas and plans for you, but it's really in their interest, not yours.

DOWNERS: These types will drag you down to doom and gloom before you have time to say "Good morning," or "Have a nice day." They generate a constant flow of problems, complaints, and doubts. They are full of tales of those who tried and always failed. Whatever you suggest, they delight in responding, "It can't be done. It won't work . . . I don't like it. It's never been done before!" Downers can make you feel like a simple-minded Pollyanna or a goody two shoes because you feel positive. The downers can inject their negative venom into your reservoir of positive goals, dissipating your energy, polluting your imagination, and weakening your resolve. Downers sabotage your goals and everything else along the way. Don't waste time and energy trying to bring them along, for they are specialists in "being down," and they will seize the opportunity to dim your light and make you wish you'd stayed in bed. For a downer the light at the end of the tunnel can only be the headlights of an oncoming train.

GUSHERS: Watch out! These types will smother you with goodies and "good intentions." They are "just trying to help. . . ." Like the manipulators, gushers have their own agenda and needs to fulfill. To meet their needs, they will skillfully, even artfully, orchestrate invitations, favors, gifts (that you don't need!), all manner of ways to "just help out." They may insist that they want nothing in return, but don't believe them. If you do get caught in the struggle to return those "kindnesses," you run the risk of feeling guilty when you can't reciprocate or even when you simply decide not to play at all. Nobody wins.

Identify the clingers who may be sapping your time, energy, and emotions. Decide on the adjustments that would be best for you. Obviously, you cannot expect a parent to stop being a parent, but it is possible to define your own priorities and ask for their understanding and support. Washington-based clinical psychologist Dr. Adi Shmueli suggests that one way to deal with clingers who may be close family members or longtime personal friends is to have a frank discussion regarding your present situation. Explain that you are working on a goal or project that is very important to you, and that you may appear to be a bit preoccupied. You don't have as much time now to spend with them to meet their expectations or needs. Shmueli suggests setting aside some "quality" time later for catching up, if you choose to. Dr. Shmueli has seen this strategy work wonders. Even overly attentive parents can accept a sincere appeal for temporary relief from their expectations.

Ideally, we should strive to preserve and maintain close personal ties but at the same time remain independent and autonomous. In the process, some clingers will have to be abandoned. Few clingers really change their expectations, so they are happier when they find someone more receptive to their particular needs and agendas.

When you feel burdened by other people and their demands, ask yourself: "Whose needs am I meeting?" If it turns out that you are meeting their needs more than your own, you had better check your life for clingers—parasites, manipulators, downers, and gushers—and take the necessary action.

1. IDENTIFY the clingers.

2. GIVE YOURSELF PERMISSION to disengage from the ones who may be taking advantage of you.
3. DECIDE on the best approach to deal with each of them. One or more of the following strategies will work:
   a. Negotiate new "terms of endearment."
   b. Begin to limit your involvement.
   c. Sever the relationship completely . . . move on.

Dr. Gerald Kushel, author of *Centering,* suggests making a list of all the people in your life and ranking them according to importance. He writes:

> Cold as it may sound, inner-liberated persons rank other people according to a hierarchy so they can avoid confusion when it comes to making certain necessary choices. They fully appreciate that they cannot be all things to all people. . . . It is wise to remind yourself periodically of your priorities in your relationships. There is no reason to mislead your friends or yourself.

Devise a method of dealing with clingers that most suits your personality and style. Granted, you are wading into sensitive waters with strong emotional undercurrents. But this is part of giving up the past. It allows you to grow up and move ahead!

◆ Listen to Winners

Just as clingers can deplete your energy, dampen your spirits, and rob you of precious time, winners can actually help you in your pursuit of higher goals. Identify yourself with positive, successful people—those who share your commitment to growth and achievement. You will experience the most exhilarating exchange of energy, ideas, admiration, encouragement, and respect in such relationships. Have you noticed how much better and confident you feel after spending time with certain individuals? Those are the people who nourish your resources, instead of depleting your energy. Watch them, listen to their positive attitudes, share your own confidence and positive personality.

I have often heard other high achievers describe the energy and inspiration they derived from other winners. It may not be an everyday occurrence, but it's worth waiting for the opportunity for an exchange of energy and ideas, a discovery of shared experiences, a new perspective, and a mutual understanding. The companionship of winners also gives you a chance to tap your own resources, stretch your imagination, and help you fully realize your potential.

Winners recognize each other. You will know and feel who they are, and they will recognize you. We all need friends and companionship. Make your friendships count. Invest time in relationships that are full of mutual growth. Cultivate friends who stretch and care for you, who contribute to your energy and inspire your best thinking, nourish your imagination and spark your vision. The fellowship of winners is an exchange of the positive and the possible. Share your best with your friends, and they will open their experience to you. Winners are a good investment!

◆ Make Way for Change

Clear the way for change. That means new experiences, new people, even a new look. Many people are afraid of change in any form. My grandmother had a fit whenever the furniture was moved, so of course my mother and Aunt Barb delighted in changing the room arrangement while Gram was shopping or working in the garden. They were convinced that a "change" would give Gram a lift, would break up the routine. As soon as we left, she promptly returned the chairs and the sofa to their designated spots. As I grew up I found that it is not unusual for people to live with an exact furniture placement for a lifetime. To them, change is disruptive and threatening. The longer they can keep things the same, the more overall control they feel they can retain over their lives. Entire lifetimes have been devoted to maintaining the status quo, which to high achievers is the antithesis of growth.

On the other hand, not all changes are the right changes.

I came to recognize much of my own restless behavior as signals indicating the need for deeper, more basic changes and reordering in my life. I would crave a new hairstyle or fashion "look." Then certain rooms began to look all wrong. Before the real source of change surfaced, I misdirected my efforts and money toward superficial "revisions." Don't get me wrong. There is nothing like a new hairstyle or dress to lift the spirits, but when those changes fail to bring more than temporary satisfaction, you may need more than a lift. A good many of the perpetual shoppers of the world shop not only out of boredom. Take it from a reformed shopper: many are really seeking change—healthy, personal growth—but they get caught on the shopping circuit and just never kick the habit. Their shopping and rearranging become another convincing method of avoiding real change.

If change is so wonderful, why is it often feared and avoided? Roger Gould, M.D., author of *Transformations,* examined the intricacies of change. Gould describes how he and his bride felt upon their marriage and new independence from their parents:

> A tether to our parents was torn, and we
> mourned it. We were a little less fettered by
> the codes of life our parents had woven into
> the tether, but we were left temporarily un-
> anchored in time and space. . . .

Giving up the past, dealing with the realities of life, is all part of what Gould describes as "the process of shedding a whole network of assumptions, rules, fantasies, irrationalities and rigidities that tie up our childhood consciousness."

◆ Never Too Late for Change

I had the privilege of interviewing William Attwood on *Today* when his book, *Making It Through Middle Age,* was released. This is a man who embraces change! Attwood was foreign editor of *Look* magazine, President Kennedy's ambassador to Guinea, President Johnson's ambassador to Kenya, editor-in-chief of Cowles Communications, and president of

Newsday, a major regional newspaper—all since his fortieth birthday! During that period he also suffered two heart attacks and was crippled by polio. He not only survived, but he overcame his disabilities and went on to meet and make changes in his life. He writes, "Every time you change jobs you meet new people, learn new things and see new sights . . . and with mobility you develop the self-confidence that comes from coping with unfamiliar situations and discovering unsuspected talents within yourself."

William Attwood lives an evolving, changing life, the kind that expands knowledge, experience, and sophistication and produces a maturity earned through conscious decision making and not annual birthdays. Attwood's brand of change assumes a natural ebb and flow. It cannot be rigidly structured but occurs in leaps and lapses, a process Dr. Roger Gould calls the "growth rhythm":

> [The growth rhythm is] dictated by pauses for rebuilding or reshaping our reality structure. . . . We get anxious when we really have moved too fast and should slow down, and also when we are about to transgress an outdated internal standard that should be disregarded.

Find the tides of your change. Flow with the changes, and rebuild and regenerate during the less active periods. Accept change as one of the permanent conditions of life. Put it to work in your behalf. Dr. Roger Gould sums it up:

> When we grow, we wander in an uncharted area. But if we wander long enough, we begin creating a new structure. That's the way we're built; there's no fighting it.

I think of change as the percussion section of this book, beating the cadence for achievement and growth. Don't get tangled in the past or have your growth entrapped in the clutching vines of clingers.

◆◆◆

Here are some reminders that will keep your drummers marching forward:

Are you suffering from "past" overload?

· Check your location. Are you stuck on a path that goes in circles? Leads to a dead end?

· Do you need to make a change announcement? If so:

   a. State concisely the changes in your life (use What, Where, Why, Who, and so on).

   b. If it would be helpful to friends and associates, go ahead and mail it out.

   c. If not, keep it as a private declaration to organize troubling ambiguities and clarify the misunderstandings that surround a recent change.

· Check your surroundings for too many moldy reminders of the past. Too much nostalgia breeds stagnation.

· Let go of old habits—make room for new behavior. You cannot be your old self and your new self at the same time.

· Initiate an anticlinger campaign. Hold an imaginary meeting of all the people in your life. Are they:

   a. Parasites?

   b. Manipulators?

   c. Downers?

   d. Gushers?

· Decide the most sensitive manner in which to deal with each. Will you:

   a. Renegotiate their role?

   b. Readjust their position?

   c. Relocate them—perhaps out of your life?

· Align yourself with winners. Make time to be with other high achievers, those who stimulate your creative energy, appreciate your abilities, stretch your mind, and share your humor, experiences, and feelings.

· Be receptive to change. Welcome life's transitions even if they occur at inconvenient times or places.

◆◆◆

Change marches beyond the past right into the future. Don't watch, *join* the parade, and remember, it's never too late! Roll your drums, crash your symbols, and move to the head of your parade. March out of the past and, to the new music of change, watch your life take off!

14

◆

Courage with a Small "c"

In human beings courage is necessary to make being and becoming possible.

—ROLLO MAY, *The Courage to Create*

COURAGE DOES NOT always have to begin with a capital "C." That's the kind of courage we bring forth for the grandiose rhetoric of commencement addresses, funeral eulogies, political speeches, and battles with terminal illnesses. Daily we hear of acts of courage by firemen, policemen, and soldiers, but few of us get credit for the simple acts of courage that move us to become fully mature. John F. Kennedy reminded us of this when he said, "We should not forget those acts of courage with which men [and women] . . . have lived."

When my older son, Jeff, was nearly nine, he came to me one morning and announced that he would be pitching his pup tent in the far corner of our property, which totaled seven and a half wooded acres, and there he would spend the night alone. Jeff set about organizing flashlight, canteen, Ritz crackers, and M&Ms for his solitary adventure in the wilds. As

I hunted for batteries and his sleeping bag, I asked why it had to be that night, and why he didn't want to have a friend over to camp out with him. He looked at me with eyes that held a universe and said, "Mom, I just want to see if I can last all night out there alone."

His answer has haunted me. He uttered the words that cry out from our very souls. How much can I take? What can I do? What are my limits? I respected his need to test his courage, but I made it clear that if he decided to come back to the house, it wouldn't mean that he'd failed. Life would bring plenty of contests. Jeff stayed in the woods all night, and he seemed quite satisfied with himself when he returned in the morning. He never talked much about it or expressed the need to repeat the experience.

We all need to test our courage. We all need to find out what we can do, how much we can take, how well we adjust, and how far we can go. It is the essential question that drives us to find out what and who we really are. What kind of person dwells inside this human casing? The answers bring us self-knowledge, self-esteem, self-acceptance, and peace. Avoiding those questions, or denying them by never probing, testing, or measuring ourselves, creates the restless anxieties of the unresolved, never-completed human being.

Many overachievers are driven by these unrelenting, unanswered questions. Too many workaholics and overachievers are on the fast track to success not because they are committed to growth, purpose, and a richer life, but because they are searching for answers to their deepest questions. Many haunted, dissatisfied, unfulfilled men and women spend a lifetime avoiding or denying their essential need to face the challenge my young son confronted: to see if they can last out there alone. Without asking and answering that question, and the litany of questions that frames our basic self-understanding, we never define ourselves. And that brings us to courage.

Testing, challenging, and measuring our own limits require enormous courage. Pride, dignity, and self-respect grow out of such courage. We don't always win all the personal contests; sometimes we have to come in early from the dark night to try again. But through the process of trying we come to know the boundaries of ourselves, the map of our own territory. You can change the boundaries, expand them, rearrange them, but knowing the quintessential self brings deep satisfaction and peace. This is the self that knows when enough money has been accumulated or enough property has been acquired. A boundary-wise seeker knows when a new goal must be set. This is the self that lives by a set of priorities and values that frees rather than enslaves, that allows a life of peace and fulfillment rather than one saddled with the priorities and agendas of others.

I've seen them. I know them. Men and women who are beaten down by a society that offers instant, superficial answers to the tormenting, urgent questions of the soul. Questions that have been muffled by money, silenced by promotions, perks, and possessions, and betrayed by false benefits and rewards. I see it in the faces of those haggard, compromised chameleons who "have it all," but who are still searching, who will die searching unless they listen to the eight-year-old within who asks: "Who am I?"

Like most women, I grew up accepting courage as an exclusive male franchise. Little girls did not have to camp out all night alone to test their courage. We read Stephen Crane's *The Red Badge of Courage* in junior high English to learn that the young male hero found his courage on a Civil War battlefield after being paralyzed by fear and wounded. Girls were expected to squeal when the lights went out, to run from bugs, and to become nauseated at the thought of dissecting the frog in biology class. We watched as the boys struggled to differentiate between real and imagined courage in the physical arenas of football and fistfights. Oh, there were Joan of Arc and Susan B. Anthony: one was burned at the stake and the other used persuasion and marched with protest signs. There wasn't much in between—no pilots, astronauts, or race-car drivers— nothing that would qualify in the traditional categories of courage. At that time, women were the objects of men's courage—to be protected by male courage. All the old clichés were at work. Would your choice of a male protector have the courage to "defend" a lady's honor? The teenage translation: Could your steady beau beat up any guy who danced too close?

Nobody ever told me that I could be courageous, or that I would need to be. Women seemed to find courage through death, disease, or hardship, and if they endured without falling apart, they were praised by being called "strong," rather than brave or courageous. Instead of finding courage in sports, games, or careers, women acquired strength through adversity—the kind most people would rather avoid.

The whole system seemed so unfair. The poor guys had to endure terrible physical punishment and the girls assumed that courage just wasn't part of their biology. Instead, a girl would reflect her partner's courage, a kind of secondhand virtue.

No one told me that decisions would call for courage. Perhaps teachers, ministers, and parents talked about "convictions, honesty, valor," but at that time it didn't translate into my young perceptions of life. That genre of courage seemed the exclusive domain of Winston Churchill and Dwight D. Eisenhower. No one told me it was an act of courage to have a child. No one told me it took courage to end an unhappy marriage or to face rejection in the marketplace.

General R. E. Chambers, former chief of the U.S. Army's psychiatry and neurological consultant division, states:

> Most people don't know how brave they are. Many potential heroes, both men and women, live out their lives in self-doubt. If they only knew they had these deep resources, it would give them the self-reliance to meet most problems, even in a big crisis.

I never knew that I had courage. Like most people, I had no battlefields, only the mundane settings of everyday situations. But the battlefields of the everyday test all our courage.

When I first moved to Buffalo, New York, to take up my work on *A.M. Buffalo,* the first month was a living hell. The demanding work, my depressing temporary accommodations, the loneliness of my daily struggles required every ounce of my courage just to keep going. At the end of August, when Billy returned from camp, I vowed to honor our annual fall custom of shopping for his new school clothes. However, my new job and the delayed move into our condominium forced me to postpone our shopping trip several weeks. When we finally did get to the shopping center it was about 8:00 P.M. Even though I was unfamiliar with the mall's many shops, I didn't think we could go wrong with its one major department store. By the time we piled the new jeans, shirts, underwear, and socks on the checkout counter, it was nearly closing time. The bill was $110.50. I had been in Buffalo two months and had established bank credentials, bought a new home, and begun my daily television responsibilities, but I still had my Ohio driver's license. The salesclerk would not accept my check. I was incredulous, angry, exhausted, and emotionally spent. That had never before happened to me. I felt more alone than ever. I wanted to cry, but Billy's inquisitive eight-year-old eyes impaled me. I had to have courage.

The salesclerk suggested that I leave the merchandise and the check and pick up the clothing when my check cleared. No. That was a direct challenge to my honesty. My son was watching to see how I would handle this. I was his sole guardian. Would I cave in under the pressure of this unpleasant salesclerk and the stares of the customers waiting behind us in the checkout line? Would he feel safe and secure with a woman who broke down and cried at the rejection of a check? I demanded to see the manager. There were several calls to the office. They had trouble locating him. Everybody wanted to go home. I held firm. Billy tugged at me. "It's okay, Mom," he said. "Let's just go home." Finally I was told to take the escalator to the second floor. The manager's receptionist greeted me, got the manager on the phone, and relayed the situation to him. He never appeared, but he instructed his receptionist to approve the check.

That incident was the beginning of a succession of new tests of my courage. I never knew that I had that kind of courage—more than the store manager! Only much later did I realize that these tests called for more than mere "strength"— we're talking about raw courage!

I think of courage as a pilot light standing ready to fire up our burners when we face the fear of indecision, new opportunities, challenges, risks, failures—all the essential raw materials of growth. It takes courage to grow up. It takes courage to decide on specific goals for ourselves; courage to persist and stick to them. As Rollo May wrote in *The Courage to Create,* "People attain worth and dignity by the multitude of decisions they make day to day. These decisions require courage. . . . It is essential to our being." In 1961, Francis Rodman wrote in the *New York Times,* "Courage does not always march to airs blown by a bugle; it is not always wrought out of the fabric ostentation wears."

Courage is seldom the brass bands and confetti that we have come to associate with heroes. It's more like the tiny, silent pilot light flickering within, ready to fire into brilliant energy and resolve when called upon to meet an awesome challenge or a quiet, private decision of principle. We all have that pilot light of courage. Too often we don't recognize it or hesitate to call it courage.

Today, both men and women are finding new definitions and realizing broader expressions of courage in their lives. One such example occurred in the unlikely arena of major corporate America, where personal sacrifice and sixteen-hour workdays are prerequisites to reaching the top.

For more than a decade John Reed had been considered a strong contender for the top position of president and chief executive office of Citicorp, the world's largest banking institution. However, in the mid-1970s Reed's wife began to suffer emotional stress from her husband's long hours and work-related travel. He had been devoting nearly all his time and effort to his banking career, leaving the management of the home and their four children to his wife. When the family began to show symptoms of trouble, Reed abruptly changed his work habits, fully aware of the possible professional consequences. Nevertheless, to the satisfaction of many, and the disbelief of some, in June 1984, Walter Wriston, chairman and CEO of Citicorp, named John Reed his successor.

The profile of Reed's "metamorphosis" from workaholic to devoted family man appeared as front-page feature profiles in *The New York Times,* the *Wall Street Journal,* and *Business Week.* In previous years, an executive's personal life was not even discussed in the office and certainly would never have been approved for release by the tightly controlled corporate public information departments. However, this report, complete with family photographs, explained that Reed was home every night by six o'clock to be with his wife and their four children. As one business associate observed, "John may have been a robot before, but suddenly he became people-oriented and sensitive." John Reed's decision to change his work habits meant risking the loss of an important goal in his life, but he had the courage to be true to his personal priorities. The best part is that he achieved his professional goal, too. In fact, one insider was quoted as noting, "Walt Wriston believes that John's recognition of his family's needs was probably the best thing that could have happened to Citicorp." Don't overlook the courage Wriston exhibited in rewarding the priorities Reed chose to follow. By his decision to name Reed his successor, and by making the Reed family open to the press, he set a precedent in corporate America.

Such courage reminds me of what Leon Blum wrote in his book *Marriage:* "I have often thought morality may perhaps consist solely in the courage to make a choice."

Over two thousand faces passed through the television lights of my career, and many more offered truths from the shadows. In each example of outstanding accomplishment it is courage that stands out as a common, constant factor. The pilot light of personal courage shines through the pages of this book. Remember Pamela Reising, who climbed a treacherous mountain to gain physical confidence, overcome her fear of heights, and become more assertive in her career. There was Jessica Mitchell, who overcame the pain and crippling effects of arthritis while remaining productive in her career as associate fashion director at Saks Fifth Avenue. Financial adviser David Elias succeeded in spite of a learning and speech disability and rejection by friends, teachers, and neighbors. Sally Raphael, the syndicated radio personality, was fired eighteen times before she became the celebrity she is today. Ice cream giant Earle Swensen was gripped with fear while he waited to see if risking his life's savings and leaving his government job would pay off in the ice cream business. Every one of them had courage—the kind that is called into action for each step toward achieving our goals. Courage is the omnipotent sustainer as we progress through challenge, risks, opportunities, and failures. It takes courage to maintain a sense of humor, to give yourself permission, to persist, to be resilient, and to let go of the past.

John F. Kennedy called courage "the universal virtue." But it is also the essential quality present in exceptional achievement. As Kennedy wrote in *Profiles in Courage*:

> To be courageous requires no exceptional qualifications, no magic formula, no special combination of time, place, and circumstances. . . . The stories of past courage can define that ingredient—they can teach, they can offer hope, they can provide inspiration. But they cannot supply courage itself. For this each man [and woman] must look into his [or her] own soul.

We all possess enormous courage. We just need to let it shine. Recognize many of your choices as courageous. Be aware of that pilot light within, and seek its flame in times of doubt and darkness. Let it carry you to decisions, accomplishments, awareness, and truths, to the goals you may never have thought possible. Dr. Maxwell Maltz tells us, "Daily living also requires courage—and by practicing courage in little things, we develop the power and talent to act courageously in more important matters."

Put your courage to work for you. And call it courage! Give yourself permission to recognize your own courage. Reward yourself for the courage you apply in daily living. For a woman it may mean the courage to choose to live alone. For a man it may mean the courage to be sensitive and loving, to cry. Courage doesn't necessarily involve other people. It can be a silent contest with the self.

Thucydides wrote, "The secret of happiness is freedom, and the secret of freedom is courage."

Discover your pilot light of courage. Put it to use. Turn

up the flame of courage in your life to illuminate the path to your goals.

◆◆◆

- Have the courage to DECIDE what you want of life. WRITE DOWN those goals.
- Have the courage to COMMIT YOURSELF to achieving your goals.
- Have the courage to prove you CAN when someone says you CAN'T.
- Have the courage to LEARN something new.
- Have the courage to GIVE YOURSELF PERMISSION, and don't wait for it from others.
- Have the courage to manage your emotions—to be angry, to be afraid, to be loving.
- Have the courage to be persistent, resilient, and to work hard.
- Have the courage to laugh at yourself and adversity.
- Have the courage to fail and to learn from failure and bounce ahead.
- Have the courage to recognize opportunities and to exploit them if they prove to be wise.
- Have the courage to TAKE CARE OF YOURSELF and give yourself a REWARD when you deserve it.
- Have the courage to LET GO OF THE PAST, to move on when it's time.
- Have the courage to deal with "clingers" who may be holding you back.
- Have the courage to adapt to change.
- Have the courage to grow and mature, to meet the future with enthusiasm and hope.

◆◆◆

♦

Conclusion

Like a newborn baby, this book came into the world without a name, and like naming a baby, everyone got into the act. We tried on dozens of titles—some were too cute, others too tough, too ponderous, or gimicky, others too feminine, frilly, or forgettable. I approached my literary agent with *How to Get from Nebraska to Network* and *From Lemon Pies to Limousines*. He said, "Look, Nancy, no one can relate to those titles. No one is going to get a job like yours. There are only two like it in the nation!" I forgot about the titles and took a moment to gloat privately. He was right; there are only two jobs like mine in the nation, but I've got one. I went after this job, and I got it. It can be done!

There are those who will say, "Oh, sure, but she was Miss Nebraska," or, "She can talk about success, but she's got looks to start with. . . ." I'll let you in on a little secret: I am very plain and ordinary-looking. My best feature is probably my thin ankles. My teeth are uneven. I have mousy brown hair.

I have small facial features, a sallow complexion, and at five two I am considered short. I put on weight just like everybody, and on a small frame it shows instantly. During the stressful period of my divorce and first television jobs, I broke out in adult acne! For months I made regular visits to a dermatologist, and with makeup covering up the painful, unsightly, swollen areas on my chin and cheeks, I went on the air; cosmetics and determination can work wonders. I just decided to make the most of what I have!

Of course there are those who choose to believe that we are on the brink of a nuclear holocaust; those who watch the environmental deterioration and predict the worst; those who insist that the economic indications point to a second great depression. Others forecast the collapse of the American family, public education, law enforcement, the international monetary system, public transportation, and democracy itself. A steady diet of news broadcasts and certain newspapers and you will begin to believe it all. Sure it's important to be an informed, responsible citizen, but that doesn't mean living a life of doom and gloom. The facts are that the health of the general population is improving, Americans are living longer, food is readily available and a bargain compared to the situation in most countries.

There are jobs for those who want to work, and there are still plenty of opportunities for the innovative entrepreneur. Free education is available to every child in this country, and the resources are available to anyone who wants to learn. There are inexpensive travel possibilities for those who are willing to look for them; as Americans we are permitted to travel around the world!

The information available in this country is mind-boggling, and most of it is free! The precious raw materials and tools for creating a productive, happy, fulfilled life are all here! The limitations, the obstacles, the reasons we think we can't succeed come from within, not from the outside. Just as no outside force is going to come along and sweep us into our success dream, no outside force can keep us from those things in life we really want. The doom and gloom movement stands ready to provide support to those who are looking for excuses, those who want to be taken care of, those who procrastinate, those who believe they can't!

The fact is everybody at any age has the capacity to grow intellectually, emotionally, and financially. Everybody has the right to get the most out of his or her life. Michael Korda, author of *Success!*, declares:

> The American dream is not dead; opportunities are still available and the ability to see one and exploit it is as important and rewarding now as it has ever been. . . . It still holds true for the person who knows how to succeed, everything represents an opportunity, even situations that at first appear to be negative.

There is no joy or growth in negativism, and eventually the miasma begins to show in a person's expression, appearance, and health. Protect your "pilot light" from the drafts of negativism; if it goes out, rekindle it.

Not long ago I received a call at my NBC office from Jim Denny, the reporter from the *Omaha World Herald* who had interviewed me in 1961, just after I had won the Miss Nebraska Pageant. Although I hadn't heard from him in years, I remembered him instantly. During our conversation, he reminded me of the quotation he had used as a headline on the feature story he'd written about me.

With notebook in hand, Jim Denny had come backstage after the pageant to get in on some of the postpageant emotion. His question zapped the euphoria and caused a flicker in the electricity of winning. "Nancy," he had asked, "aren't you concerned that your size will hinder your chances in Atlantic City?" (A pause to relight the pilot light!) My response was the caption: "I may be small, but I have big ideas!"

Those big ideas have been the most important energy force in my achievements, and I plan to keep them working for me.

◆ How Do You Eat an Elephant?

To take on the world, to tackle all the principles of success set forth in this book, may seem overwhelming, and rightly so. I learned about them over a lifetime! Then I spent several years observing, testing, categorizing them. Don't attempt to achieve all your goals tomorrow. Don't think that you can clean the garage, write a goal contract, learn to give yourself permission, practice visualization, begin your notebook of cartoons, cut down on fattening foods, run a mile a day, shed a clinger, and reward yourself all in one day! You will be exhausted, frustrated, and discouraged.

This is the time to take a tip from the elephant joke "How do you eat an elephant?" Answer: "One bite at a time." How do you climb a mountain? One step at a time. How do you build a house? One brick at a time. The truly permanent structures are built deliberately, methodically, over time. Lifelong habits cannot be changed overnight, and certain ideas, views of life cannot be changed by quickly reading a book. The steps of success can most certainly change your life for the better, but you must start with one brick, one step, one bite, and each day take another one, then another. Before you know it, you've devoured the beast!

Try this plan. Reread chapter 1 on setting goals and work on that chapter for one month. The next month read chapter 2 and concentrate on those principles while keeping up the commitments you have made to your goals. Each month read the next chapter, and concentrate on adding the next step to your success repertoire. And you're on your way—bound for success. The chapters are cumulative and contagious; each discovery, each successful initiative moves you forward. You will find each one connecting and integrating to build a pathway to new confidence in yourself and your future. At the end of the year you will have mastered the steps.

◆ Review and Renew

From time to time we all need a refresher, a boost to get things back on track. Just pick up this book and return to the chapter that deals with the faulty or weakening link. Then draw support, energy, and confirmation from the lessons, anecdotes, advice, and genuine caring you will find. Consider this book a winner you can turn to when things get cloudy and you need inspiration and a push.

As this book progressed, it took on a life of its own and became a profoundly illuminating experience for me. Although it was sometimes wrenching to revisit and share my own experiences, I was moved and encouraged by those of others. *Bound for Success* became my personal "outward bound." Let it be yours!